7MINUTES
WITH **GOD**
DAILY DEVOTIONS FOR A DEEPER RELATIONSHIP

7MINUTES WITH GOD

DAILY DEVOTIONS FOR A DEEPER RELATIONSHIP

FEATURING THE MESSSAGE® //REMIX™

TH1NK
P.O. Box 35001
Colorado Springs, Colorado 80935

ISBN 1-57683-813-7

Cover design by Mattson Creative
Cover photo by Getty Images
Creative Team: Gabe Filkey, s.c.m., Laura Wright, Arvid Wallen, Kathy Mosier,
    Pat Reinheimer

Printed in Canada

1 2 3 4 5 6 7 8 9 10 / 09 08 07 06 05

CONTENTS

INTRODUCTION 6

WEEK 1:
CREATIVE 8

WEEK 2:
PASSIONATE 22

WEEK 3:
POWERFUL 36

WEEK 4:
FRIGHTENING 50

WEEK 5:
NEAR 64

WEEK 6:
SILENT 78

WEEK 7:
JUST 92

WEEK 8:
MERCIFUL 106

WEEK 9:
TRUTHFUL 120

WEEK 10:
FAITHFUL 134

CONTRIBUTORS 148

INTRODUCTION

And now for something completely different . . .

You know what to expect in a devotion.

A little Bible verse.
A little story.
A little prayer.
A little time with God.

You can zip through it in less time than it takes for the marshmallows in your Lucky Charms to turn the milk in your cereal bowl a really funky color.

As soon as you turn the page, you may think this devotion is no different. After all, it won't bombard you with a ton of words on every page. You can read each of these seventy devotions in about seven minutes or less. Hence the title, 7 Minutes with God.

But this book in your hands is not the same-old, same-old. For one thing, the devotions don't start with you. They start with God. Each week you will explore a different aspect of the character of God your Father. For another thing, each week is put together so that no two days are alike. On the first day, you will read the Bible to get you thinking about the topic for the week. Another day you will focus on prayer. Another on praise. Another on taking action based on what you've read. You'll even be challenged to fast once a week, but no two fasts are alike. Skipping a meal or two is just one way to do it.

Each week also includes a reflection on the week's topic by a student from Azusa Pacific University. These students have put on paper some of the things you think but never believed anyone would put into words. They have also written many of the other daily devotions. To learn more about these students, check out the contributors section at the end of the book.

The final devotion each week is primarily a bunch of blank lines waiting for your writing. We didn't run out of things to say and therefore decide to use the lines to fill space. The lines are there for you to journal your thoughts from the week. As you consider the character of God, what do you want to say to Him in response? Tell Him in this journaling section.

We didn't write this devotion to give you seventy pithy thoughts. Instead, we want your Bible reading and prayer and fasts to be launching points for conversations between you and God that last much longer than seven minutes each. Our goal is to help you think through your faith. In the end, as you come to see your faith through God's eyes, we hope the way you see your world changes.

This devotion is different. It is different by design. And by the time you get to the end, we pray you will be different too.

Mark Tabb, general editor

CREATIVE

"If you decide for God, living a life of God-worship, it follows that you don't fuss about what's on the table at mealtimes or whether the clothes in your closet are in fashion. There is far more to your life than the food you put in your stomach, more to your outer appearance than the clothes you hang on your body. Look at the birds, free and unfettered, not tied down to a job description, careless in the care of God. And you count far more to him than birds.

"Has anyone by fussing in front of the mirror ever gotten taller by so much as an inch? All this time and money wasted on fashion—do you think it makes that much difference? Instead of looking at the fashions, walk out into the fields and look at the wildflowers. They never primp or shop, but have you ever seen color and design quite like it? The ten best-dressed men and women in the country look shabby alongside them.

"If God gives such attention to the appearance of wildflowers—most of which are never even seen—don't you think he'll attend to you, take pride in you, do his best for you?"

BIBLE READING

//REFLECT

We usually hear only one command in these verses: Don't worry. But I want you to focus on what else Jesus told us to do. We will spend this week walking in the fields and looking at the wildflowers. No, this isn't your first foray into life as a botany major. Instead, it's an excursion to see the artistry of God. When He created the universe, He didn't just make it functional like a well-oiled machine. He filled it with beauty.

As we come face-to-face with the creative genius of our God, we will discover His thumbprint on our own lives. Every time we draw a picture or write a story or mow designs into the outfield at a ballpark, we express the creative image of God within us.

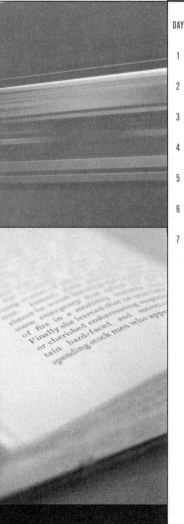

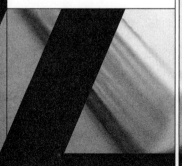

CREATIVE

//PSALM 19:1-6

God's glory is on tour in the skies,
God-craft on exhibit across
the horizon.
Madame Day holds classes every
morning,
Professor Night lectures each
evening.

Their words aren't heard,
their voices aren't recorded,
But their silence fills the earth:
unspoken truth is spoken
everywhere.

God makes a huge dome
for the sun—a superdome!
The morning sun's a new husband
leaping from his honeymoon
bed,
The daybreaking sun an athlete
racing to the tape.

That's how God's Word vaults
across the skies
from sunrise to sunset,
Melting ice, scorching deserts,
warming hearts to faith.

//PRAY

You, O God, are an awesome
and holy God who loves and
continually blesses Your children.
You are powerful and amazing.
The artistry of Your creation
stirs my heart, even though my
small mind can't fathom the
vast universe You spoke into
existence. All of creation gives
You praise and honor! Day after
day and night after night, Your
glory and amazing love show
through all that You have made.

PRAYER & SOLITUDE

//THINK

- What does the beauty of creation tell me about God?
- What will happen to my focus if I learn to seek God's artistry in everything?

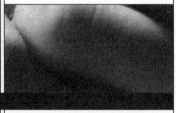

I cannot hide from You, for You are everywhere and You show up in everything I do. O God, I long for You to be the focus of my life instead of my focus being the temporary material objects I crave. Fix my heart on You. Open my eyes to see all You have blessed me with. Make me more grateful for the things I take for granted. Lord, please humble me. Focus all my attention on You so I don't focus on myself. Draw me away from my meaningless possessions and closer to Your side.

Lord, I pray that You will be glorified every day through Your incredible universe. You are the awesome Maker, and I pray that those who don't know You will see Your amazing grace and magnificence through creation. I pray that someday everyone will see Your beauty. O God, You are the reason I breathe, for no one is greater or more loving than You. I praise You for the wonder of Your grace and kindness.

Tiffany Jean BeMent
Age: 18
Major: business marketing

CREATIVE

//ROMANS 11:34-36

Is there anyone around who can
explain God?
Anyone smart enough to tell him
what to do?
Anyone who has done him such
a huge favor
that God has to ask his
advice?

Everything comes from him;
Everything happens through him;
Everything ends up in him.
Always glory! Always praise!
Yes. Yes. Yes.

FASTING

//REFLECT

God made everything. He wrote
the laws of physics that determine
how fast the sun burns its fuel,
how far the Earth stays from
the sun, and everything else
that makes life possible in this
universe. God designed you down
to the simplest cells you had to
study in biology. All that stuff
about mitosis and meiosis and
everything else that takes place
inside your body on a cellular
level—God thought it up and
made it all work on His first try.
No trial and error for God. Nor is
there anything simple in even the
simplest parts of creation. From
a quantum level to the farthest
ends of space, all of it works with
a precision the human mind will
never fully understand.

So why do we think we can give
God advice? We do it all the time.
We offer God advice every time
we complain about the way our
lives are going and every time
we offer Him a helpful hint of
how things could be done better.

//FAST

I do it. You do it. We all do it. We try to make our words sound religious, but the bottom line is still this: We who cannot figure out how a brown cow can eat green grass and produce white milk try to boss around the God who designed hydrogen atoms and oxygen atoms in such a way that two of one and one of the other make water.

Today, take a fast from telling God what He should do. Spend time in prayer, but do not tell God what He should do or how He should do it. No "and make my chemistry professor have a flat tire today so I won't have to take that test I didn't study for" prayers. Instead, ask for the wisdom to see His handiwork in your life and for the grace to accept those situations you would rather He obliterate. Then spend time praising Him and thanking Him. Replace complaints with praise. God knows what He's doing. As you fast today, let that truth fill your heart.

CREATIVE

ACTION

//GENESIS 1:1-3,6-7,9,11

First this: God created the Heavens and Earth—all you see, all you don't see. Earth was a soup of nothingness, a bottomless emptiness, an inky blackness. God's Spirit brooded like a bird above the watery abyss.

God spoke: "Light!"
    And light appeared. . . .

God spoke: "Sky! In the
        middle of the waters;
    separate water from water!"
God made sky. . . .

God spoke: "Separate!
    Water-beneath-Heaven,
        gather into one place;
Land, appear!"
    And there it was. . . .

God spoke: "Earth, green up!
    Grow all varieties
of seed-bearing plants,
Every sort of fruit-bearing
        tree."
    And there it was.

//REFLECT

The story keeps going. God speaks and creation springs into being. Of course, we don't hear the background story, but we know it's there. Before God speaks, He plans His masterpiece down to the last detail. And it all fits together perfectly with incredible beauty and amazing precision.

Nor do we hear the inflection in God's voice as He creates. When producers of those church dramas (in which everyone dresses in his bathrobe) recruit someone to play God, they usually pick a person with a deep, stern voice. While the voice of God must have boomed with majesty on each of the six days of creation, stern doesn't seem like the right adjective to describe it. Reread the first chapter of Genesis and see if you don't detect joy in God's voice. Making everything is not a chore, like cleaning your room or dragging the trash can to the curb. No, all of this is great fun for God. You can almost hear Him laugh and sing as He spins the stars like a top in the Milky Way and paints the rings around Saturn.

//ACT

Today your assignment is simple: Go have fun creating something. Draw a picture or write a story or plant a garden. Make something. Anything. Finger paint or sculpt your mashed potatoes into a castle or invent a new pasta sauce. Write some jokes or build a barn or knit a sweater for your dachshund. Whatever you do, express the creative image of God in you and have fun doing it! Be original. Be creative. Be like God.

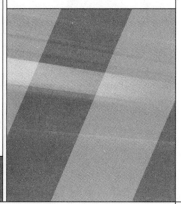

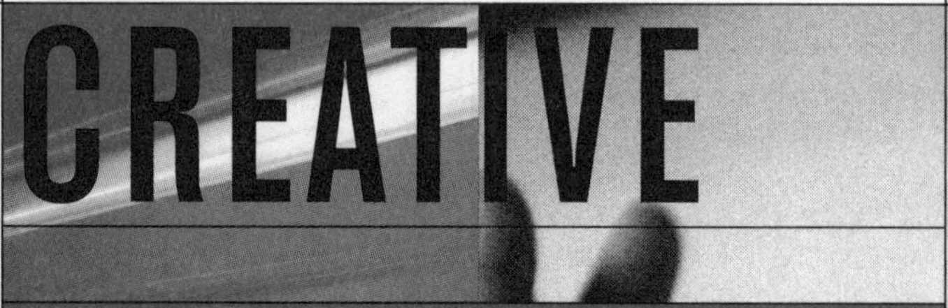

CREATIVE

//PSALM 33:1-3 AND EXODUS 15:1-2

PSALM 33:1-3

Good people, cheer God!
Right-living people sound
best when praising.
Use guitars to reinforce your
Hallelujahs!
Play his praise on a grand
piano!
Invent your own new song to
him;
give him a trumpet fanfare.

EXODUS 15:1-2

Then Moses and the Israelites sang this song to God, giving voice together,

I'm singing my heart out to
God—what a victory!
He pitched horse and
rider into the sea.
God is my strength, God is
my song,
and, yes! God is my
salvation.
This is the kind of God I have
and I'm telling the world!
This is the God of my
father—
I'm spreading the news far
and wide!

PRAISE &
CELEBRATION

//REFLECT

When God does something great, we want to hold on to the moment and never forget it. On top of our praise and celebration, we also want to tell the rest of the world what our God has done for us. We want everyone to know how wonderful and magnificent our God really is. Sure, we're bragging, but that's okay. God doesn't mind when we brag about Him.

In the Bible, people wrote songs to do this. These songs were passed on from one generation to the next so that the nation would never forget what God had done. The Exodus passage you just read is the first few lines of one of these songs. Moses and the Israelites sang it the day God parted the Red Sea for them.

//CELEBRATE

You don't have to be a songwriter to sing a new song to God. All you have to do is think back on everything He has done for you, write it down, and then sing it back to Him. That's your assignment for today. Invent a new song for God. No one else has to hear it. After all, it's God's song. He's the only audience that matters. The style of the song can be whatever you want, from classical to country to rock to rap. It doesn't even have to have much of a tune; just a chant will do. A song filled with praise to God for all He's done always sounds sweet to His ears. Whatever style you choose, the point is to fill this song with praise for specific things God has done for you. Then sing it to this audience of One.

CREATIVE

But the basic reality of God is plain enough. Open your eyes and there it is! By taking a long and thoughtful look at what God has created, people have always been able to see what their eyes as such can't see: eternal power, for instance, and the mystery of his divine being. So nobody has a good excuse. What happened was this: People knew God perfectly well, but when they didn't treat him like God, refusing to worship him, they trivialized themselves into silliness and confusion so that there was neither sense nor direction left in their lives. They pretended to know it all, but were illiterate regarding life. They traded the glory of God who holds the whole world in his hands for cheap figurines you can buy at any roadside stand.

MY JOURNEY

//MY GOD

So many times I search for God and miss the evidence of His presence, which He has placed right in front of my nose. God's handiwork shines in everything from the precise alignment of the planets to the incredible work ethic of the ant. If we fallen humans would only stop and see what's there, we would find God's love all around us, drawing us near and showing us His power and might.

This is especially true for Christians. We experience His wonder yet become complacent and restless in our faith. I know I do. So often I'm like the people of Romans who exchanged God's glory for meaningless junk. Even though I claim that Jesus is the most important Person in my life, I get caught up in chasing the next best thing in fashion or electronics or you name it. Sometimes I'm so completely wrapped up in the stuff of this world that I completely miss what God has given me for free—the wonder of creation and the grace of His love.

//MY THOUGHTS

- How do I see God through His creation?
- What can I do to stay away from worshiping meaningless things?
- What can I do to see God more often and more easily?

Caylee Carpenter
Age: 18
Major: psychology

//MY PRAYER

I pray that I would stop being so wrapped up in myself that I miss the amazing wonder of God. I pray that I would stop settling for things that satisfy me for only a short time. I pray that I would never grow complacent in my time spent with God because God deserves my everything. Anything less is just a waste.

//JOURNALING: PSALM 19:1

God's glory is on tour in the skies,
God-craft on exhibit across
the horizon.

As you gaze at the artistic wonder God puts on display in His creation, what do you learn about His character? What will you do in response? How will you change your life in light of who God is?

PASSIONATE

GOD's Message came to me. It went like this:

"Get out in the streets and
     call to Jerusalem,
   'GOD's Message!
I remember your youthful
     loyalty,
   our love as newlyweds.
You stayed with me through
     the wilderness years,
   stuck with me through all
     the hard places.
Israel was GOD's holy choice,
   the pick of the crop.
Anyone who laid a hand on
     her
   would soon wish he
     hadn't.'"
     GOD's Decree.

Hear GOD's Message, House
     of Jacob!
   Yes, you—House of
     Israel!

GOD's Message: "What did
     your ancestors find fault
     with in me
   that they drifted so far
     from me,
Took up with Sir Windbag
   and turned into windbags
     themselves?
It never occurred to them to
     say, 'Where's GOD,
   the God who got us out of
     Egypt,
Who took care of us through
     thick and thin, those
     rough-and-tumble
   wilderness years of
     parched deserts and
     death valleys,
A land that no one who
     enters comes out of,
   a cruel, inhospitable land?'

"I brought you to a garden
     land
   where you could eat lush
     fruit.

BIBLE READING

But you barged in and
        polluted my land,
    trashed and defiled my dear
        land.
The priests never thought to
        ask, 'Where's GOD?'
    The religion experts knew
        nothing of me.
The rulers defied me.
    The prophets preached god
        Baal
And chased empty god-
    dreams and silly god-
    schemes."

//REFLECT

You know God is love. God loves you. God loves me. God loves everybody because God loves the world. But do we ever step back and see Him as a real lover, someone who puts His heart on the line for those He loves? God is love. Somehow when we throw these two words together, we often forget the emotion—the passion—wrapped up in His love.

Read today's Bible verses again. Read them until you feel the pain God felt when His first love turned her back on Him and started messing around with other lovers. Put yourself in God's place. What would you do if the one to whom you'd pledged your undying love did to you what Israel did to God? What then does it mean to love Him?

PASSIONATE

//ROMANS 5:7-8

We can understand someone dying for a person worth dying for, and we can understand how someone good and noble could inspire us to selfless sacrifice. But God put his love on the line for us by offering his Son in sacrificial death while we were of no use whatever to him.

//REFLECT

I have always struggled to comprehend the everlasting love of our God. How could One so wonderful, so perfect, love me? I am nothing but a speck in this vast universe. And I am weak. My desires and my passions for worldly indulgences overcome me far more than I want to admit. And yet He still loves me.

I feel guilty for the sins I commit, but I still run back to them because I enjoy them. It's a never-ending cycle of sin, guilt, prayer, and hope that one day I will be forgiven. Then I read verses

PRAYER & SOLITUDE

Dear Lord, please help me to know Your everlasting love. Help me to avoid temptation. Help me to remember that I am and always will be a sinner and that You already know and accept this. No matter how unclean I am, I will always be Your daughter and servant. Help me to remember those who suffer more than I do and to recognize that my life is blessed. And lastly, help me to share Your love with everyone I know.

like these and remember that He already knows what I've done. He sees all my sins. He knows that I never have been and never will be perfect. And yet His amazing love is still there.

I guess I may never understand this unfailing love. So I must believe that He will protect me from those things that hurt me and leave me weary. I must believe that He will guide me away from the misleading arms of temptation and toward better paths. And above all, I must believe that He will pick me up when I fall, dust me off, and tell me, *It's all right. I still love you. Keep going. I'm right behind you, and I always will be.*

//THINK

- Am I alone in my struggle to understand God's love? What will I do to comprehend His undying love in my life?
- Am I forgiven for all of my sins? Why? How?

Jennifer Tibbett
Age: 18
Major: English

PASSIONATE

//MY FOCUS: 1 JOHN 4:16

We know it so well, we've embraced it heart and soul, this love that comes from God.

God is love. When we take up permanent residence in a life of love, we live in God and God lives in us.

MY JOURNEY

//MY GOD

I recently experienced God's love in a way that rocked my world. Last summer I went on a mission trip with forty other students to the poverty-stricken Andros Island, Bahamas. Before leaving, we prepared a shipment of supplies with pretty much everything we might need: food, water, Bible lessons, paint, tools, craft supplies, games, and more. This shipment was scheduled to arrive the same day we did. Shortly after we got there, we set up camp while our youth pastor went to retrieve our supplies. Six hours later he returned with nothing. The boat had problems and could not depart. Our shipment was never going to get there.

What were we going to do? This was the question we were all asking. Then God stepped in. We had our mouths, we had our Bibles, and we had God. Specifically, we had His love, which was supposed to be our reason for being on

Andros in the first place. We didn't need any other supplies to share His love with the people.

I experienced the act of living in love that week. God's love and passion made it possible for me to love those kids and teach them all I know about Christ. We weren't able to build or paint, but we made a lasting impact. Love was what the people of Andros needed, and God gave it to them through our mission team.

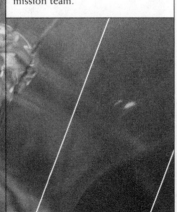

//MY PRAYER

I desire to be a living representation of Christ's love. I pray that I may walk in *His* love and not *my* love. I pray that I may understand the true meaning of His passion and love for me. I want to become as passionate about God as He is about me.

//MY THOUGHTS

- How have I allowed God's passion for me to help me overcome my limitations?
- How will I share His great love with others on a daily basis?

Michelle Galloway
Age: 18
Major: undeclared (probably art)

PASSIONATE

//ROMANS 12:1

So here's what I want you to do, God helping you: Take your everyday, ordinary life—your sleeping, eating, going-to-work, and walking-around life—and place it before God as an offering. Embracing what God does for you is the best thing you can do for him.

PRAISE & CELEBRATION

//REFLECT

See that verse there? I've been familiar with it for a long time. It's one of the first Bible verses I ever learned. But until recently, I never really thought about what it means. It tells me to take everything I have, everything I am—even my body—and offer it to God as a living sacrifice.

Lots of people argue about what kinds of postures and physical expressions should be encouraged in worship. For me, this verse sums it up. My whole body belongs to God, and He deserves nothing less than my whole body in worship. What does that mean? Should I lift my hands? Should I kneel and bow? Should I dance? Should I find some sort of altar and lie down on it (you know, like a sacrifice)?

Here's where it all starts to make sense for me: Jesus took on flesh—a body, something that was new for Him—and then He laid down that body as a sacrifice. It was His offering to His Dad.

Please excuse this choice of words, but when it comes to worship, what would Jesus do? He would lay down everything in obedience. Not just His singing voice, not just His 10 percent in the offering plate, but His very body and life. He passionately gave everything, and He expects the same from me. A passionate God deserves passionate worship.

//PRAISE

Are you holding back in your worship of God? Are you worried about what others might think? Do your praises reflect passion for Jesus, or do you simply go through the motions? Worship isn't confined to an hour on Sunday. It's a way of life, every day laying down your body as an offering to God. Find a creative way to do this today. You may need to actually lie down on the floor and tell God, *Here I am. I'm all Yours.* Then, as you go through the rest of the day, think of yourself as a sacrifice on an altar to God and allow Him to do what He wills. In everything you do, express praise and thanks to Him.

Ross King, contributing editor

PASSIONATE

ACTION

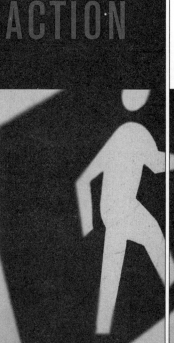

//1 JOHN 4:20-21

If anyone boasts, "I love God," and goes right on hating his brother or sister, thinking nothing of it, he is a liar. If he won't love the person he can see, how can he love the God he can't see? The command we have from Christ is blunt: Loving God includes loving people. You've got to love both.

//REFLECT

If love is truly pure, then shouldn't it be about *who* instead of *what*? I want to love people for who they are rather than what they are. I can love my parents, my teachers, and even my friends without ever knowing about their sexual preferences. Why should the sexual activities of the homosexual friends, teachers, and family members in my life keep me from loving them? God's love is unlimited; shouldn't mine be as well? If there were no labels, I could love people for who they are rather than what they do when I am not around.

Beauty lies in the eye of the beholder, and as the beholder of my world, I pray I will see the beauty in everyone around me. My hope is to love like the God who loves all and to accept people in whatever way, shape, or form they come.

//ACT

Look at the people in your life. Look beyond your friends and see the people God keeps sticking in your path. Write down the names of the individuals you find hard to love. Look especially at those whose lifestyles keep you from loving them.

You know what's coming, don't you? Do something tangible today to show God's love to those people. Praying for them from a distance doesn't count. You have to actively show them God's love in a way that forces you to step out of your comfort zone.

//THINK

- How do my actions and words limit God's love?
- Do I believe God really loves those who do things He hates? Why or why not?
- How does God love people without accepting everything they do? How can I?

Darrah Christel
Age: 18
Major: marketing

PASSIONATE

//MARK 12:29-31

Jesus said, "The first in importance is, 'Listen, Israel: The Lord your God is one; so love the Lord God with all your passion and prayer and intelligence and energy.' And here is the second: 'Love others as well as you love yourself.' There is no other commandment that ranks with these."

//REFLECT

Jesus doesn't mince words in this passage. He calls His people to love God like God already loves them. The passionate God wants His children to give Him all of their love, all of their passion, all of their mind, and all of their energy in order that they may draw near to Him.

So what keeps me from fully loving God? The answer isn't someone or some material thing, although I would like to say it is. The main hindrance to my love of God is my love of me. Jesus knows this. That's why He told His disciples, "If anyone would come after me, he must deny himself and take up his cross and follow me" (Mark 8:34, NIV). So how do I do this? How do I deny the part of myself that I choose to love instead of God?

//FAST

God has made it clear to me that my selfish ambition cuts off my access to Him. For me to love my Abba with all of my passion, I have to slam the brakes on the selfish drive that wants to put myself first.

All of us are different. You are the only one who knows what pulls your heart away from truly loving and following Christ. So the first step for you in today's fast is to spend time alone with God and ask Him, *What one thing in my life keeps me from loving You with all of my passion?* Once you know the answer (and you probably know it already), fast from this one thing for the rest of the day. When continuing the fast feels like a sacrifice, keep at it. Even after this fast is over, keep examining your heart. Every day ask yourself, *Am I answering His call to love?*

Corrie Brazell
Age: 20
Major: English

//JOURNALING: 1 JOHN 3:16

This is how we've come to understand and experience love: Christ sacrificed his life for us. This is why we ought to live sacrificially for our fellow believers, and not just be out for ourselves.

No one can experience God's love and not be changed by it. How has your understanding of God's love and passion for you changed this week? How does your life need to change as a result? Whom does God want to love through you?

POWERFUL

//GENESIS 1:1 AND REVELATION 19:11-16

GENESIS 1:1

First this: God created the Heavens and Earth—all you see, all you don't see.

REVELATION 19:11-16

Then I saw Heaven open wide—and oh! a white horse and its Rider. The Rider, named Faithful and True, judges and makes war in pure righteousness. His eyes are a blaze of fire, on his head many crowns. He has a Name inscribed that's known only to himself. He is dressed in a robe soaked with blood, and he is addressed as "Word of God."

The armies of Heaven, mounted on white horses and dressed in dazzling white linen, follow him. A sharp sword comes out of his mouth so he can subdue the nations, then rule them with a rod of iron. He treads the winepress of the raging wrath of God, the Sovereign-Strong. On his robe and thigh is written, KING OF KINGS, LORD OF LORDS.

BIBLE READING

//REFLECT

You'll need to pull out your Bible for today's devotion. Read Genesis 1. As you do, underline the phrase "God spoke" whenever you come across it. Before God spoke, nothing existed. Then He spoke and *BAM!* instant universe! That's the power God wields. He merely speaks a word, and whatever He says happens.

Next read Revelation 19. This chapter tells what happens on the last day of earth's history. Every army in the world stands ready to fight against Jesus. They've amassed every weapon mankind has ever invented and are ready to fire toward the sky. How does Jesus fight back? He doesn't. He speaks. That's what the phrase "a sharp sword comes out of his mouth" means. Jesus speaks and the battle is over.

This week we will explore the power of our God. His power is absolute. He can do anything He wants to do. Nothing can stop Him. We will see God's power unleashed in stories such as the Creation and the parting of the Red Sea. As we do, we will be left with a question: How does God put His power on display today?

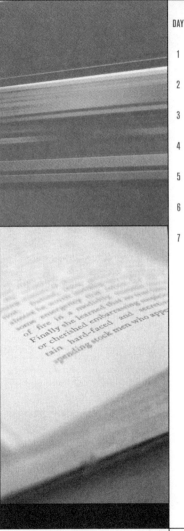

POWERFUL

1 CORINTHIANS 1:18-19,22-24

The Message that points to Christ on the Cross seems like sheer silliness to those hellbent on destruction, but for those on the way of salvation it makes perfect sense. This is the way God works, and most powerfully as it turns out. It's written,

> I'll turn conventional wisdom
>   on its head,
> I'll expose so-called experts
>   as crackpots. . . .

While Jews clamor for miraculous demonstrations and Greeks go in for philosophical wisdom, we go right on proclaiming Christ, the Crucified. Jews treat this like an *anti*-miracle—and Greeks pass it off as absurd. But to us who are personally called by God himself—both Jews and Greeks—Christ is God's ultimate miracle and wisdom all wrapped up in one.

ROMANS 1:16

It's news I'm most proud to proclaim, this extraordinary Message of God's powerful plan to rescue everyone who trusts him, starting with Jews and then right on to everyone else!

PRAISE & CELEBRATION

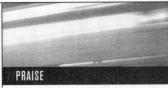

//REFLECT

People wonder why God doesn't do anything extraordinary today. *Where is the power?* they ask. *Where are the miracles like we read in the Bible?* These two passages tell us God's power is right in front of us. Every time someone hears the good news of Jesus, God's power surrounds him. And every time someone responds to this news by asking Jesus to become his Savior, the ultimate miracle takes place. The new believer passes from eternal death to eternal life. Both today and forever change. That's power.

//PRAISE

Too often we praise God only when He does something in our own lives or when we see Him do something in the world so far over the top, so dramatic, that we have to break out in applause. Today, look at the lives of other believers you know. Ask them to tell you how they were saved and what their lives were like before that. Some of the stories may be pretty spectacular. Others will sound ordinary. Pay attention to them all. As you listen, look closely at how God's power has changed these lives.

The rest of your assignment is to praise God for the way His power has changed your life and the lives of people around you. Let other people in on what you are doing. Throw a party to celebrate the power of the good news of Jesus!

POWERFUL

EXODUS 14:27-31

Moses stretched his hand out over the sea: As the day broke and the Egyptians were running, the sea returned to its place as before. GOD dumped the Egyptians in the middle of the sea. The waters returned, drowning the chariots and riders of Pharaoh's army that had chased after Israel into the sea. Not one of them survived.

But the Israelites walked right through the middle of the sea on dry ground, the waters forming a wall to the right and to the left. GOD delivered Israel that day from the oppression of the Egyptians. And Israel looked at the Egyptian dead, washed up on the shore of the sea, and realized the tremendous power that GOD brought against the Egyptians. The people were in reverent awe before GOD and trusted in GOD and his servant Moses.

EXODUS 15:22-24

Moses led Israel from the Red Sea on to the Wilderness of Shur. They traveled for three days through the wilderness without finding any water. They got to Marah, but they couldn't drink the water at Marah; it was bitter. That's why they called the place Marah (Bitter). And the people complained to Moses, "So what are we supposed to drink?"

FASTING

//FAST

Even when we don't complain to God directly, all our grumbling is really aimed at Him. Every time we gripe, we say, *God, why won't You do anything to fix this?!* For the next twenty-four hours, remove whining from your vocabulary. Don't complain about the weather or a professor or the food in the cafeteria. Whenever you feel a gripe forming on your tongue, find something to praise God for instead. Complaining is the opposite of faith. Today, walk by faith, not by sight. Pray and sing praises rather than whining. God and the people around you will appreciate the change.

//REFLECT

Three days. That's how long it took the Israelites to go from singing God's praises for parting the Red Sea to grumbling against Him for letting them run out of drinking water. Apparently they had short memories. After all, did they really think the God who opened up a sea would now let them die of dehydration? Yet most of us aren't so different. Think back over the past several months. Have you seen God work in your life in an unmistakable way? How long did it take you to go from praising Him to complaining?

POWERFUL

Hell is ripped open before God,
graveyards dug up and
exposed.
He spreads the skies over
unformed space,
hangs the earth out in empty
space.
He pours water into cumulus
cloud-bags
and the bags don't burst.
He makes the moon wax and
wane,
putting it through its phases.
He draws the horizon out over
the ocean,
sets a boundary between
light and darkness.

Thunder crashes and rumbles in
the skies.
Listen! It's God raising his
voice!
By his power he stills sea
storms,
by his wisdom he tames sea
monsters.
With one breath he clears the
sky,
with one finger he crushes
the sea serpent.
And this is only the beginning,
a mere whisper of his rule.
Whatever would we do if he
really raised his voice!

MY
JOURNEY

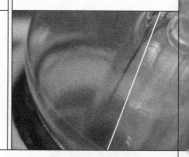

//MY PRAYER

My God, I pray that I will be forever in awe of Your sovereign rule and the power of Your whispers. I don't want to listen to my own voice. I pray that I will gratefully submit to and seek Your voice, knowing that it is supreme. I praise and give thanks to You for Your powerful love that is present in my life. You give me the peace of knowing that You and You alone will tame the monsters in my life.

//MY GOD

At some time in your life you were probably around a man with a voice so powerful that it made all the neighborhood kids stop playing and all the adults turn around and look. The voice may have been comforting, or it may have been frightening. But you listened because it was one of those voices no one could ignore.

That's how God's voice is. With it, He controls nature, opens hell, creates the skies, rules the oceans, and tames monsters. "And this is only the beginning, a mere whisper." God will gladly use His powerful voice in our lives, whether we seek it ourselves or He steps in uninvited for our own good. He loves us so much that He will use the same power He used to create the heavens and the earth to intervene in our lives and tame our monsters.

//MY THOUGHTS

- What happens when I seek my own foolish voice instead of God's supreme voice?
- How will I listen for God's voice in everything I do?

Leslie Joy Randleman
Age: 20
Majors: communications; psychology

POWERFUL

ACTION

//EPHESIANS 1:17-21

But I do more than thank. I ask—ask the God of our Master, Jesus Christ, the God of glory—to make you intelligent and discerning in knowing him personally, your eyes focused and clear, so that you can see exactly what it is he is calling you to do, grasp the immensity of this glorious way of life he has for Christians, oh, the utter extravagance of his work in us who trust him—endless energy, boundless strength!

All this energy issues from Christ: God raised him from death and set him on a throne in deep heaven, in charge of running the universe, everything from galaxies to governments, no name and no power exempt from his rule. And not just for the time being, but *forever*.

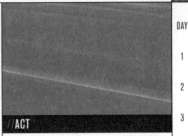

//REFLECT

I cringe at the idea of people looking at me as their only or best reflection of who God is. What if I mess up? What if they see me at my worst and think God isn't real because of me? This responsibility makes me want to crawl into my little Christian hole and never come out. Maybe that way no one will be turned off to Christ because of my poor portrayal of Him.

But then I read, "Oh, the utter extravagance of his work in us who trust him—endless energy, boundless strength!" and I wonder why I would ever think that my influence as a Christian has anything to do with me. This verse allows me to walk with new faith that the light inside of me can't be hidden despite myself because my God is the God who runs the universe, because my God is in control of all things. How can I be afraid to fail when His arms hold me up? My smallness melts into His greatness, and amazing things will be accomplished through my small life with His great power.

//ACT

Has God shown you a task He wants you to do, but you've been afraid to try it? Today, risk failure and do it. Take a stand for God. Tell a friend about Jesus and explain how she can be saved. Don't worry about failing. Don't worry about looking like a loser. Trust God's power, feel His arms around you, and act. Saying you believe that God is all-powerful doesn't mean a thing if you are afraid to let His power flow through you.

Rebecca Joy Burton
Age: 20
Major: communications with an emphasis in journalism

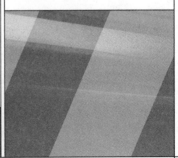

POWERFUL

//PSALM 2:1-6

Why the big noise, nations?
Why the mean plots, peoples?
Earth-leaders push for position,
Demagogues and delegates meet
    for summit talks,
The God-deniers, the Messiah-
    defiers:
"Let's get free of God!
Cast loose from Messiah!"
Heaven-throned God breaks out
    laughing.
At first he's amused at their
    presumption;
Then he gets good and angry.
Furiously, he shuts them up:
"Don't you know there's a King
    in Zion? A coronation
    banquet
Is spread for him on the holy
    summit."

//REFLECT

God totally ripped me open this summer. Even though I'd gone to church and read His Word my whole life, I kept doing little things to mess it up. Then one day in July, I *really* messed up. I engaged in acts with a girl that I'd never planned on doing outside of the confines of marriage. I became broken. I could not function. Not so much because I was embarrassed or thought no one else had ever done that before but because I felt scared and disappointed in myself. God, the only God, *my* God, has done so much for me, and yet by doing

PRAYER & SOLITUDE

//PRAY

Get alone with God and ask Him to open your eyes to your mistakes. Look long and hard at those areas where you struggle and at the things you've done that you can't tell anyone about. Then look at the power of our God. Ask Him for the help you need. Ask Him to change you.

Remember that God loves you and will never abandon you—even when you blow it.

Adam Cozens
Age: 20
Major: media communications

what I did, I spat in His face. Did I forget there's a King in Zion? Why would the all-powerful Lord of the universe take such abuse from an insignificant person like me?

But through my tears (and trust me, there were lots of them) and through my screaming at the top of my lungs for it all just to go away, I discovered the greatness of God's healing power. My God cared enough about me to ease my hurt, dry my tears, and forgive my sin. I was overwhelmed with joy! This sounds like a stereotypical Christian message, but I don't want it to be taken as that. God changed me, and He will change you too. We all mess up, but sometimes our mistakes are what allow us to see most clearly.

//JOURNALING: JOB 26:12-16

By his power he stills sea storms,
   by his wisdom he tames sea
      monsters.
With one breath he clears the
      sky,
   with one finger he crushes the
      sea serpent.
And this is only the beginning,
   a mere whisper of his rule.
   Whatever would we do if he
      really raised his voice!

What would you do if God really raised His voice? As you catch a small glimpse of His power, how does your understanding of God need to change? How does your life need to change?

FRIGHTENING

// 2 SAMUEL 6:3-11

They placed the Chest of God on a brand-new oxcart and removed it from Abinadab's house on the hill. Uzzah and Ahio, Abinadab's sons, were driving the new cart loaded with the Chest of God, Ahio in the lead and Uzzah alongside the Chest. David and the whole company of Israel were in the parade, singing at the top of their lungs and playing mandolins, harps, tambourines, castanets, and cymbals. When they came to the threshing floor of Nacon, the oxen stumbled, so Uzzah reached out and grabbed the Chest of God. GOD blazed in anger against Uzzah and struck him hard because he had profaned the Chest. Uzzah died on the spot, right alongside the Chest.

Then David got angry because of GOD's deadly outburst against Uzzah. That place is still called Perez Uzzah (The-Explosion-Against-Uzzah). David became fearful of GOD that day and said, "This Chest is too hot to handle. How can I ever get it back to the City of David?" He refused to take the Chest of GOD a step farther. Instead, David removed it off the road and to the house of Obed-Edom the Gittite. The Chest of GOD stayed at the house of Obed-Edom the Gittite for three months. And GOD prospered Obed-Edom and his entire household.

BIBLE READING

//REFLECT

Most of us are like Uzzah. We treat God with far too little respect. Uzzah touched the Chest of God, the physical representation of God's presence and holiness to the Old Testament nation of Israel, even though God said that should never be done. And Uzzah died as a result. We read the story and think God is unfair, which makes us miss the point.

We can approach God only on His terms. He is holy. He is mighty. He spoke the universe into existence, and one day He will speak it out of existence. And He makes the rules. David became angry with God for striking down Uzzah, but David should've been angry at himself. He approached God far too casually and treated His commandments like suggestions. Once David experienced the awesome power of God, he was filled with fear.

The Bible says, "The fear of the LORD is the beginning of wisdom" (Psalm 111:10, NIV). This week we will look closely at the awesome might of God and come away afraid. At least we should.

FRIGHTENING

ACTION

//MARK 4:35-41

Late that day he said to them, "Let's go across to the other side." They took him in the boat as he was. Other boats came along. A huge storm came up. Waves poured into the boat, threatening to sink it. And Jesus was in the stern, head on a pillow, sleeping! They roused him, saying, "Teacher, is it nothing to you that we're going down?"

Awake now, he told the wind to pipe down and said to the sea, "Quiet! Settle down!" The wind ran out of breath; the sea became smooth as glass. Jesus reprimanded the disciples: "Why are you such cowards? Don't you have any faith at all?"

They were in absolute awe, staggered. "Who is this, anyway?" they asked. "Wind and sea at his beck and call!"

//REFLECT

We rarely think about God as being powerful. Instead, most people see Him as nothing more than a lovable teddy bear. God's power is on display throughout the Bible, but we don't seem to get it. These verses from Mark are a perfect example. Jesus got up and told the wind and the waves to knock it off. If I had been in that boat, I don't know what I would have been thinking, but one thing is certain: I would have been scared to death seeing that kind of power from the guy in the front of the boat.

//ACT

When we get a grip on God's power, we will have the same kind of fear. This fear comes out in our lives as respect. Most of us don't show God enough respect, but we should. That's how we show God we really love Him.

Before you do anything today, stop and ask yourself, *How does this show my respect for God?* Examine the way you talk and the way you treat other people (especially those in authority). Think about how you can show God proper respect in everything you do today. Then do it. Let the fear of God overflow into your everyday life. Take a long, hard look at His power and authority. If you really believe He is who He says He is, let your actions show it.

Andrew Wheeler
Age: 20
Major: communications with an emphasis in journalism

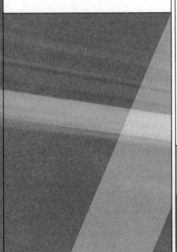

FRIGHTENING

//EXODUS 20:18-20

All the people, experiencing the thunder and lightning, the trumpet blast and the smoking mountain, were afraid—they pulled back and stood at a distance. They said to Moses, "You speak to us and we'll listen, but don't have God speak to us or we'll die."

Moses spoke to the people: "Don't be afraid. God has come to test you and instill a deep and reverent awe within you so that you won't sin."

//REFLECT

The private Christian high school I attended had a chapel speaker who often preached on hell and coming judgment but seldom on grace. Sometimes, especially during the weeks when students were caught out of dress code or playing pranks or rumored to have been drinking alcohol, the chapel speaker urged us to come up front, kneel down, repent, and be saved.

For whatever reason, I couldn't go up front. And as I sat with my head bowed, I questioned my salvation even though I knew I was a Christian. I began to fear that I was going to go to hell or that I would be punished. *Maybe*

PRAYER & SOLITUDE

//PRAY

My prayer is that I will recognize God's absolute power and *want* to obey Him. I don't want my fear of God to equal fear of punishment or hell. I want to be so close to Him that I feel a sinking in my heart when I know He's disappointed in me.

Justin Crutchfield
Age: 21
Majors: cinema; English

God will make me homeless, I thought, or maybe my dad or mom will die so God can wake me up. I felt so wicked I couldn't even pray or talk about God.

I had the wrong kind of fear of God. It was the same fear the Israelites had after they heard God thunder out the Ten Commandments. They stood in terror, bewildered and confused, like I did in the back of chapel. Moses had to comfort the Israelites and explain the magnificent display of thunder and lightning. God was not trying to tell them He was going to smite them if they broke His commandments. He was showing them His authority and giving them a fear that would inspire reverence of His ultimate power. As a result, they wouldn't want to sin and forfeit the love He had for them — the love worth more than their lives.

FRIGHTENING

GOD is serious business.
  He won't be trifled with.
He avenges his foes.
  He stands up against his
    enemies, fierce and
    raging.
But GOD doesn't lose his temper.
  He's powerful, but it's a
    patient power.
Still, no one gets by with
  anything.
  Sooner or later, everyone
    pays.
Tornadoes and hurricanes
  are the wake of his passage,
Storm clouds are the dust
he shakes off his feet.
He yells at the sea: It dries up.
  All the rivers run dry.
The Bashan and Carmel
  mountains shrivel,
  The Lebanon orchards
    shrivel.
Mountains quake in their roots,
  hills dissolve into mud flats.
Earth shakes in fear of GOD.
  The whole world's in a panic.
Who can face such towering
  anger?

MY JOURNEY

//MY GOD

I don't know whether to be comforted or scared out of my mind. What happened to the gentle Shepherd who guides His flock? What about the lap that is home to many children or the Teacher who leads millions of followers? Where is the fine line between the God who dries rivers and shrivels mountains and the God who welcomes anyone looking for help? How can I be sure I am one He wants to help and not condemn?

I know I should fear God because of His great power, but at the same time I know He is just and loves me very much. Instead of being afraid, I will take comfort in knowing that I am in the shelter and protection of the almighty God. All that tries to haunt me will have to answer to Him. And in that I find true comfort!

//MY PRAYER

I pray that I will live a life that pleases God every day. I want to be an example to those who don't know about His unfailing love. Even though He has the power to destroy, I pray that I will remember He is just and that I will live my life accordingly. I want people to look at my life and see that I am different, and I want them to ask why.

//MY THOUGHTS

- In what ways do I fail to fear God or give Him the respect He deserves?
- In light of knowing I belong to God, what in my life should I change because it doesn't please Him?

Lindy Hunker
Age: 20
Major: communications

FRIGHTENING

//ISAIAH 6:1-5

In the year that King Uzziah died, I saw the Master sitting on a throne—high, exalted!—and the train of his robes filled the Temple. Angel-seraphs hovered above him, each with six wings. With two wings they covered their faces, with two their feet, and with two they flew. And they called back and forth one to the other,

> Holy, Holy, Holy is GOD-of-the-Angel-Armies.
> His bright glory fills the whole earth.

The foundations trembled at the sound of the angel voices, and then the whole house filled with smoke. I said,

> "Doom! It's Doomsday!
>   I'm as good as dead!
> Every word I've ever spoken is tainted—
>   blasphemous even!
> And the people I live with talk the same way,
>   using words that corrupt and desecrate.
> And here I've looked God in the face!
>   The King! GOD-of-the-Angel-Armies!"

FASTING

58

//FAST

Isaiah couldn't tame his tongue, but he found hope anyway. God gave it to him. God offers us the same hope. Just as God cleansed Isaiah's speech (see Isaiah 6:7), He can cleanse yours. But you have to take it one day at a time.

Today, fast from sins of speech. Don't cuss. Don't gossip. Don't make wisecracks in the middle of chemistry that you know will disrupt class. Don't tell off-color jokes or make cutting remarks that tear people down. Every fast forces you to depend on God and the power of the Holy Spirit, and today is no exception. You can't do this, but God can if you let Him.

//REFLECT

When Isaiah came face-to-face with the holy God, he became acutely aware of how the words he used displeased God. Isaiah is in good company. That's where most of us trip up. We can keep our hands to ourselves, and we can even train our eyes not to roam where they shouldn't, but the tongue is a different story completely. From profanity to gossip to just saying the wrong thing at the wrong time, our words betray the faith in God we profess. James said, "You can tame a tiger, but you can't tame a tongue — it's never been done" (3:7-8).

FRIGHTENING

//1 KINGS 18:36-39

When it was time for the sacrifice to be offered, Elijah the prophet came up and prayed, "O GOD, God of Abraham, Isaac, and Israel, make it known right now that you are God in Israel, that I am your servant, and that I'm doing what I'm doing under your orders. Answer me, GOD; O answer me and reveal to this people that you are GOD, the true God, and that you are giving these people another chance at repentance."

Immediately the fire of GOD fell and burned up the offering, the wood, the stones, the dirt, and even the water in the trench.

All the people saw it happen and fell on their faces in awed worship, exclaiming, "GOD is the true God! GOD is the true God!"

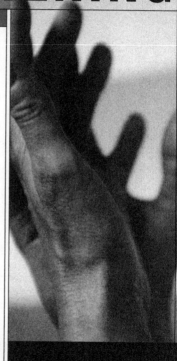

PRAISE & CELEBRATION

//REFLECT

What does it take to get you to worship? I'm not asking what it takes to get you to sing songs in church. What does it take to get you to fall on your face in absolute awe of God? You may not know the answer because you may never have worshiped God in this way. I'm not talking about the typical gather-round-the-guy-with-the-guitar-and-sing-"Kumbaya" kind of worship. Instead, falling on your face before God happens when the thought of His glory and majesty so overwhelms you that your knees give out.

//WORSHIP

I don't know if you can tell people to focus so intently on God's majesty that they nearly lose their breath, but I'm going to try. Reread today's Scripture passage and let the weight of it hit you. You may need to read the rest of the chapter in your Bible. Try to put yourself on the mountain with Elijah, the prophets of Baal, and the huge crowd of the undecided. Listen to the false prophets cry out to their gods. Imagine how bored you would be after listening to that for hours. By the time Elijah's turn rolled around, would you really expect something to happen? Probably not. Then let yourself hear the thunder crack and feel your eyebrows singe as fire falls from the sky. In that moment, what emotions would sweep through your body? How would you feel about God? How would you worship Him?

This isn't a rhetorical exercise. Today is all about praise and celebration. As you encounter the frightening Lord of the universe, worship Him.

/JOURNALING: PSALM 111:10

The good life begins in the fear
   of GOD—
Do that and you'll know the
   blessing of God.
His Hallelujah lasts forever!

The fear of God is the beginning
of the good life, the beginning of
wisdom. Why? How will your life
as a Christian change when you
get a grip on the fear of God?

NEAR

// GENESIS 39:1-7,10-14,19-23

After Joseph had been taken to Egypt by the Ishmaelites, Potiphar an Egyptian, one of Pharaoh's officials and the manager of his household, bought him from them.

As it turned out, GOD was with Joseph and things went very well with him. He ended up living in the home of his Egyptian master. His master recognized that GOD was with him, saw that GOD was working for good in everything he did. He became very fond of Joseph and made him his personal aide. He put him in charge of all his personal affairs, turning everything over to him. From that moment on, GOD blessed the home of the Egyptian—all because of Joseph. The blessing of GOD spread over everything he owned, at home and in the fields, and all Potiphar had to

concern himself with was eating three meals a day.

Joseph was a strikingly handsome man. As time went on, his master's wife became infatuated with Joseph and one day said, "Sleep with me." . . .

She pestered him day after day after day, but he stood his ground. He refused to go to bed with her.

On one of these days he came to the house to do his work and none of the household servants happened to be there. She grabbed him by his cloak, saying, "Sleep with me!" He left his coat in her hand and ran out of the house. When she realized that he had left his coat in her hand and run outside, she called to her house servants: "Look—this

BIBLE READING

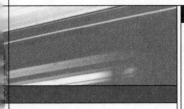

//REFLECT

Hebrew shows up and before you know it he's trying to seduce us. He tried to make love to me but I yelled as loud as I could." . . .

When his master heard his wife's story, telling him, "These are the things your slave did to me," he was furious. Joseph's master took him and threw him into the jail where the king's prisoners were locked up. But there in jail GOD was still with Joseph: He reached out in kindness to him; he put him on good terms with the head jailer. The head jailer put Joseph in charge of all the prisoners—he ended up managing the whole operation. The head jailer gave Joseph free rein, never even checked on him, because GOD was with him; whatever he did GOD made sure it worked out for the best.

Life didn't exactly turn out the way Joseph had dreamed. He never imagined his own brothers would sell him as a slave, nor did he expect to end up in prison for doing the right thing. Joseph wouldn't have chosen any of the twists and turns life took him on. But wherever he was and whatever situation he found himself in, Joseph always had one constant in his life: God was with him.

Jesus made a promise to His disciples shortly before He left this world that He would be with them always (see Matthew 28:20). His promise outlived those who originally heard it, for He is with us today. God is always near. This week we will explore the ways in which God reveals His nearness and the change His presence makes in our lives. God isn't far away. All you need, wherever you may be, are the eyes of faith to see Him.

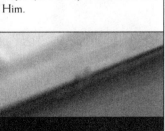

NEAR

ACTION

A hurricane wind ripped through the mountains and shattered the rocks before GOD, but GOD wasn't to be found in the wind; after the wind an earthquake, but GOD wasn't in the earthquake; and after the earthquake fire, but GOD wasn't in the fire; and after the fire a gentle and quiet whisper.

When Elijah heard the quiet voice, he muffled his face with his great cloak, went to the mouth of the cave, and stood there. A quiet voice asked, "So Elijah, now tell me, what are you doing here?"

//REFLECT

There's nothing like that last night at Christian camp. Everybody leaves so pumped up for God, though no one really remembers what the speakers said. The same is true of a True Love Waits conference or a big Christian concert. You might still have the T-shirt, but probably the only thing you remember from the event is how close you felt to God. You were excited, whether it was because of the message or the music or just standing shoulder to shoulder with friends. And you were going to hold on to that feeling of God's presence forever.

But what happens? Memories fade as life returns to the same old routine. You go back to school or work, and before you know it, you've lost that feeling of God's presence. Do you need to schedule another road trip to the next conference to get back to God? Is God near only when you feel Him?

//ACT

God promises to stay with us, even when we don't feel His presence (see Matthew 28:20). Today, look for God wherever you may be: at church, with your friends, even sitting in traffic. Rather than searching for a tingling feeling down your back, focus your attention on God Himself. How will you know if you see Him? Look for signs of His faithfulness to the promises He makes in the Bible. For example, Jesus said His Father takes care of the sparrows. So if you see a bird eating something, you witness God in action as He provides for the bird's basic needs.

God stays close to us whether we feel it or not. Pray that you will always know the truth of God's nearness in your heart when you are singing worship songs with a big crowd or sitting alone on your sofa.

Christel Kopitzke
Age: 22
Major: youth ministry

NEAR

//JOHN 14:16-17

"I will talk to the Father, and he'll provide you another Friend so that you will always have someone with you. This Friend is the Spirit of Truth. The godless world can't take him in because it doesn't have eyes to see him, doesn't know what to look for. But you know him already because he has been staying with you, and will even be *in* you!"

PRAISE & CELEBRATION

//REFLECT

Because of God's love for us, He gave us His Spirit, and His Spirit lives inside all who believe in His Son. Whenever we wonder if God is near, there's our answer. Yes, God is near. His Spirit is inside us. That's about as near as you can get.

I experience the closeness of God's Spirit as I worship. Because I lead worship for a living, I get to see God's people worshiping almost every day. And when I'm onstage with my guitar, singing and praising God, I'm constantly asking Him to move through the crowd. I pray that He will work and heal and convict and do whatever He wants to do. As I pray these things, I almost always think about the Holy Spirit. Why? Because the Spirit is near me. The Spirit is in me and on me and all around me.

It's easy for me to fall into the trap of believing that God is way off somewhere in the universe, sitting on a throne and watching the world like a giant looking down on ants. But when I think about the Spirit, I know He is near. And when I worship, I meet with Him. I speak to Him. I wait to hear from Him. And I thank Him for living in me.

//WORSHIP

Jesus said real worshipers will worship in Spirit and in truth (see John 4:24). Today I want you to lose yourself in the Spirit as you worship God. Start singing, either by yourself or in a crowd or with a worship CD, and don't worry about the words and the notes. Ask the Holy Spirit to move in your heart. Feel His presence. Experience His closeness. You don't have to scream His name for Him to hear you. He is right in the room with you. Today, worship the God who is near in Spirit and in truth.

Ross King, contributing editor

NEAR

//EXODUS 14:10-12,15

As Pharaoh approached, the Israelites looked up and saw them—Egyptians! Coming at them!

They were totally afraid. They cried out in terror to GOD. They told Moses, "Weren't the cemeteries large enough in Egypt so that you had to take us out here in the wilderness to die? What have you done to us, taking us out of Egypt? Back in Egypt didn't we tell you this would happen? Didn't we tell you, 'Leave us alone here in Egypt—we're better off as slaves in Egypt than as corpses in the wilderness.'" . . .

GOD said to Moses: "Why cry out to me? Speak to the Israelites. Order them to get moving."

//REFLECT

I've been there. I've never seen the trackless wilderness that flanks the Red Sea, but I've found it isn't necessary to travel halfway around the world just to get lost. In the hot, dusty silences between where I've been and where God is leading me lies a desert every bit as barren as the one the Israelites crossed on their way out of Egypt. For me, this desolate place is filled with unanswered questions: Where will I attend college? What am I going to major in? What career should I choose? Whom shall I marry? Where does God

PRAYER & SOLITUDE

//PRAY

God is with us, but our fears often keep us from seeing Him. Pray for the assurance that the God who brought you here has done so for a purpose. Pray also for the patience to wait for Him to reveal His plan in His time. And pray for the courage to rest securely in His plan and the promise of His closeness no matter what you go through today.

Amy Joy Serry
Age: 22
Major: chemistry

fit into all of this? I trap myself between the fathomless sea of my uncertainties and the thundering chariots of my anxious thoughts.

God, why did You bring me here? I thought I heard Your call, and yet I can't find any trace of You. Did You lead me this far just to abandon me in the desert? Why didn't You just leave me where I was? At least I was used to it. Where are You, Lord?

But God always answers. Can you hear Him? *Hush, My child. Don't you see? I've been here all along. I brought you to this place for a purpose. Stop yelling and listen. Today I am going to reveal My glory through your life. So get moving!*

NEAR

//MY FOCUS: PSALM 139:1-6

GOD, investigate my life;
    get all the facts firsthand.
I'm an open book to you;
    even from a distance, you
        know what I'm thinking.
You know when I leave and
        when I get back;
    I'm never out of your sight.
You know everything I'm going
        to say
    before I start the first
        sentence.
I look behind me and you're
        there,
    then up ahead and you're
        there, too—
    your reassuring presence,
        coming and going.
This is too much, too
        wonderful—
    I can't take it all in!

MY JOURNEY

//MY GOD

I can be totally in love with the Lord one day, and then the next I am at a party, sipping from my friend's beer or lusting after the boy next door. I have rarely experienced true physical consequences of my actions. I've never had a hangover. I've never had an STD. And I've never gotten caught. Yet.

But I have suffered the outcome of my mistakes, even if it isn't the kind that shows up in a doctor's lab report. Distance from the Lord is the consequence of my sin. How can I see the glory of God in my life if I choose to push Him away? When I sin, I fall away from the Lord, and the separation brings pain, loneliness, and indifference.

The best part about it, though, is that the Lord does not separate Himself from me. He never leaves. Instead, I can feel Him pulling me toward Him with His unconditional grace and affection. He never abandons me, even when I feel I have lost touch with Him. He knows the deepest part of my heart, and that's where He continues to work, even when I don't want Him to.

//MY THOUGHTS

- How does sin cause me to become indifferent to the love of God?
- Why do I think God seems to separate Himself from me when I need Him most? (The fact is that God will never leave us. It's the sin in our lives that blinds us to the yearning of our Lord for us.)

Carrie Taylor
Age: 21
Major: communications with an emphasis in journalism; cognate in writing and editing

//MY PRAYER

Lord, I know You are near me. Bring me close to You, even when I fall away. I pray that the desires of my flesh would not separate me from Your grace. Show Yourself to me, God, when I feel indifferent or lonely. Help me to realize that You are always there, preparing my heart to love You and be loved by You.

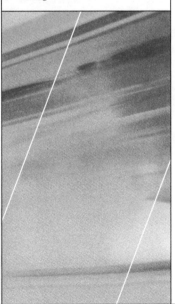

NEAR

Meanwhile, the moment we get tired in the waiting, God's Spirit is right alongside helping us along. If we don't know how or what to pray, it doesn't matter. He does our praying in and for us, making prayer out of our wordless sighs, our aching groans. He knows us far better than we know ourselves, knows our pregnant condition, and keeps us present before God. That's why we can be so sure that every detail in our lives of love for God is worked into something good.

FASTING

//REFLECT

When my grandpa was in the hospital after a heart attack, my family faced some hard decisions. We had to decide whether to keep him on life support or take him off with only a small chance of survival. Over the next week we spent time in the waiting room and at his bedside, lost between prayers for what we wanted and prayers for what would be best for him.

I have come to believe that in our loss for words, we were in the greatest position to receive God's comfort. Coming to God with no requests or expectations allowed us to grieve and hope in His presence. As much as we wanted guidance, God provided us with comfort and a chance to be together as a family. The promise of God through Christ is one of hope, peace, and comfort. It is one that allows us to draw near to God in our pain.

//FAST

Today, fast from the easy answers and quick clichés we throw out when people around us hurt and we want to avoid an uncomfortable situation. Listen to your friends and classmates as they tell you about their day or about the problems they face. Don't dismiss their pain as trivial. Instead, empathize with them. Hurt with them. Listen to them. As you listen, pray. Don't pray for the right words to say. Instead, pray for the people and the problems they dump on you. If God gives you something to say, use it. But do what James says: "Be quick to listen [and] slow to speak" (1:19, NIV). Remember, we are most connected with the suffering of those around us when we pray a prayer of tears and grief for another's pain.

Anonymous

//JOURNALING: PSALM 34:18

If your heart is broken, you'll
      find GOD right there;
if you're kicked in the gut, he'll
      help you catch your breath.

God isn't just close by. He's right
there when we need Him most.
How does His presence enable
you to face any challenge life
throws your way? He often draws
near to us through people. Is there
anyone in your life who needs a
fresh touch from God? What will
you do about that?

DAY

1

2

3

4

5

6

7

SILENT

PSALM 13

Long enough, GOD—
 you've ignored me long
  enough.
I've looked at the back of your
  head
 long enough. Long enough
I've carried this ton of trouble,
 lived with a stomach full of
  pain.
Long enough my arrogant
  enemies
 have looked down their
   noses at me.

Take a good look at me, GOD,
 my God;
 I want to look life in the eye,
So no enemy can get the best
 of me
 or laugh when I fall on my
   face.

I've thrown myself headlong
  into your arms—
 I'm celebrating your rescue.
I'm singing at the top of my
  lungs,
 I'm so full of answered
  prayers.

PSALM 22:1-8

God, God . . . my God!
Why did you dump me
 miles from nowhere?
Doubled up with pain, I call
 to God
 all the day long. No answer.
  Nothing.
I keep at it all night, tossing
 and turning.

And you! Are you indifferent,
 above it all,
 leaning back on the cushions
  of Israel's praise?

BIBLE READING

We know you were there for our parents:
    they cried for your help and you gave it;
    they trusted and lived a good life.

And here I am, a nothing—an earthworm,
    something to step on, to squash.
Everyone pokes fun at me;
    they make faces at me, they shake their heads:
"Let's see how GOD handles this one;
    since God likes him so much, let *him* help him!"

//REFLECT

I've heard my entire life how God is as close as a prayer. Preachers and Sunday school teachers and student leaders have drilled into my head the idea that God actively involves Himself in my day-to-day life. And I believe them. But what about those days when I cry out to God and He doesn't respond? I want answers, but all I hear is silence. Does God's silence mean He's turned His back on me? That's the question of the week. The answer is not as easy as you might think.

SILENT

GOD, are you avoiding me?
Where are you when I need
you?

//REFLECT

Why does God do that? Whenever I have something truly important to pray about, it seems as though He's not even listening. Sometimes I get so frustrated with Him. He wants me to come to Him with my problems, but when I do, He seems to ignore me! I can feel myself pulling away from God at these times. I'm getting back at Him, I suppose.

But why? Why would I pull back? He's answered so many of my prayers, and the few times He responds with silence, I throw a fit. I even yell at Him in my anger and demand an answer. I know that's me being human, but I also know that I should believe in Him more. Deep down I wonder if my impatience keeps Him from answering me. I'm afraid I'm only making matters worse.

PRAYER & SOLITUDE

//SOLITUDE

Today, find a quiet place where you won't be disturbed. Make a list of prayers you feel God has ignored, those you continue to pray today and those from your past. How have you reacted to His silence? What do you think God is trying to teach you through this silence? Look carefully at the list of unanswered prayers. How is your life different today because of God's silence? Talk this over with Him. As you consider the unanswered prayers from your past, can you see why God did not give you what you wanted?

//THINK

God's timing is different from our own. It's not that He isn't there; He's just making us wait until He's ready to answer. So I'm learning to be more patient. After all, He's been consistently patient with me. I should probably show Him the same respect. He's given me so much, and what can I offer Him? Nothing but my faith and love. I suppose that's enough. I know it is, even though I have a hard time making my love and faith as unconditional as His. I know that through His silence, God is showing me that He's answering with the best possible timing and in the best possible way.

Rachel Fagg
Age: 18
Major: liberal studies

SILENT

//PSALM 22:1-3

God, God . . . my God!
Why did you dump me
    miles from nowhere?
Doubled up with pain, I call to
    God
    all the day long. No answer.
        Nothing.
I keep at it all night, tossing and
    turning.

And you! Are you indifferent,
    above it all,
    leaning back on the cushions
        of Israel's praise?

FASTING

//REFLECT

Sometimes it seems as if God just isn't there. During my hardest trials when I need to know His direction and feel His guidance, I can't hear His voice. I feel like David when he cried out to the Lord and He did not answer. I scream at God, "Why don't You answer? Why do I feel so hopeless and alone? How can I understand Your plan?"

I can relate to David's psalms. I know how he felt—abandoned and ignored. Even then, David waited on the Lord and put his trust in Him, knowing that God would always take care of him and protect him, even in silence. In those moments David also put everything else aside to seek God. When times grew desperate enough, he didn't even eat.

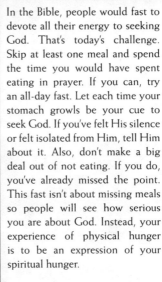

//FAST

In the Bible, people would fast to devote all their energy to seeking God. That's today's challenge. Skip at least one meal and spend the time you would have spent eating in prayer. If you can, try an all-day fast. Let each time your stomach growls be your cue to seek God. If you've felt His silence or felt isolated from Him, tell Him about it. Also, don't make a big deal out of not eating. If you do, you've already missed the point. This fast isn't about missing meals so people will see how serious you are about God. Instead, your experience of physical hunger is to be an expression of your spiritual hunger.

God uses times of silence to draw us to Him. In those moments we must exercise complete blind faith that God hears us. Do not become discouraged through God's silence but become stronger by putting your whole life in His hands. We need to be as committed as Jesus was and trust our Father unconditionally, even when we feel as though we're wasting our time.

Emily Radonich
Age: 18
Major: business administration

SILENT

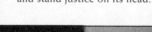

ACTION

// HABAKKUK 1:2-4

GOD, how long do I have to cry
      out for help
   before you listen?
How many times do I have to
      yell, "Help! Murder! Police!"
   before you come to the
      rescue?
Why do you force me to look
      at evil,
   stare trouble in the face day
      after day?
Anarchy and violence break out,
   quarrels and fights all over
      the place.
Law and order fall to pieces.
   Justice is a joke.
The wicked have the righteous
      hamstrung
   and stand justice on its head.

//REFLECT

Last year I saw tragedy for the first time. A friend of mine was shot and killed. He was only seventeen years old, and he had so much potential. He would have done wonderful things with his life. The person who shot him got caught, but will his punishment be equal to his crime? Even though he's in jail, he's still alive and able to talk to his family. Where is the justice?

As I write this, children around the world are being abused. The abuse will affect them for the rest of their lives. They might even grow up learning to mistreat others. Most of the people who do the abusing will walk away unpunished. Where is the justice?

//ACT

In these times of distress and injustice, where is God? The answer might surprise you. The Bible says we represent God on earth (see 2 Corinthians 5:20). When God speaks, He speaks through us. The only way, then, that God can be silent is if we are silent.

Isaiah 1:17 says,

> "Learn to do good.
> Work for justice.
>   Help the down-and-out.
> Stand up for the homeless.
>   Go to bat for the
>   defenseless."

That's your assignment for today. Find some way to stand up for the cause of justice. Help those the system has trampled. Go to bat for those who can't defend themselves. I know you can't change the world in one day, and I'm not asking you to go to Washington and talk to the president personally. Injustice doesn't have to be big to be wrong. Look for small ways you can help those who have suffered at the hands of others. And then do something. If you and I don't, who will?

Diana Robles
Age: 19
Major: psychology

SILENT

//HEBREWS 11:1-2

The fundamental fact of existence is that this trust in God, this faith, is the firm foundation under everything that makes life worth living. It's our handle on what we can't see. The act of faith is what distinguished our ancestors, set them above the crowd.

PRAISE & CELEBRATION

//REFLECT

Faith is about believing even when we can't see. Whether we talk about Hebrews 11 or the words of Jesus or even the trials of the Old Testament prophets, we find that faith is about unseen things.

But what about un*heard* things? Is faith also about singing and worshiping even when we can't hear? I think it is. I think God wants us to believe Him—believe *in* Him—no matter what our senses tell us, no matter what our tangible experience is. Faith is about believing even in the midst of silence.

So often I worship hoping that God will show me something. I hear people say, "I came to church today to hear from God." I guess there's nothing wrong with that, but I know that in my life, God doesn't always talk when I want Him to or in the way that I want Him to. Sometimes He just wants me to worship Him whether He shows me anything or not. Sometimes He just wants me to sing out in faith!

He's not being mean. I promise. In fact, He's being the loving Father He has promised to be. Faith is really important to Him, and if He always shows me and tells me everything, when will I use faith? He knows I need faith. He knows that without it, I can't make it in His kingdom.

Real faith is believing even when God is invisible. Maybe real worship is believing even when God is silent.

//WORSHIP

Worship God even if you can't hear His voice. Don't worry about feeling or hearing anything special from Him. Worship God by faith even if He is silent. Tell Him how much He means to you. Praise Him for His power and majesty. Thank Him for something He did for you today, even if you can't feel His presence. Whether you sing a song of praise or just fall down on your face before Him, worship by faith. Don't depend on what you can see or hear. Depend on the One who is greater than our ability to sense His presence.

Ross King, contributing editor

SILENT

//MY FOCUS: JOB 23:8-10

I travel East looking for him—I
    find no one;
    then West, but not a trace;
I go North, but he's hidden his
    tracks;
    then South, but not even a
    glimpse.

But he knows where I am and
    what I've done.
    He can cross-examine me all
    he wants, and I'll pass
    the test with honors.

//MY GOD

When God doesn't react to my prayers in what I feel is the appropriate time, I get discouraged. If He loves me so much, why is He taking His time? I want action. It's so hard to be patient. I'm not here long enough to be completely comfortable with God's timeline. I may not be around to see my prayer answered. And by then I will have lost my faith in God.

He wouldn't let that happen, would He? This is the problem I face. This is where my distrust of His overall plan comes from. Even though He may act in a roundabout way, I can't see it. I get the impression that God has forsaken me. I don't think I'm the only person who feels this way.

MY JOURNEY

//MY PRAYER

Let me have the patience to follow You and never stray. As I walk along the straight and narrow, I see many diversions. I can easily get distracted. I could use some horse blinders as well.

It's so hard to understand that God has His own plan and that His plan is better for me than my quick fix. I have to trust in God even when I don't understand. His answer seems to come so much faster when I'm not waiting for it. Think of painting a house. I could sit around and watch the paint dry. But what's the use? It will dry even if I'm not there. And I get more done that way.

//MY THOUGHTS

- If God is all around, why do I so often feel alone?
- When I speak during these times, how will I know I am heard? Will God answer? How can I believe He will?
- Does God have to answer for me to continue to trust in Him? Why or why not?

Brian Allan
Age: 19
Major: undeclared (maybe art, maybe writing, maybe nothing)

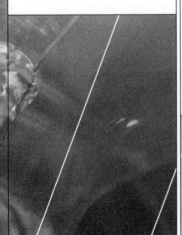

//JOURNALING: AMOS 8:11-12

"I'll send a famine through the
     whole country.
   It won't be food or water
        that's lacking, but my
        Word.
People will drift from one end of
     the country to the other,
   roam to the north, wander to
        the east.
They'll go anywhere, listen to
     anyone,
   hoping to hear GOD's
        Word—but they won't
        hear it."

Has God ever been silent in your life? What do you think He was trying to teach you through His silence? Did it work? What have you learned through the experience? If you have come away bitter and angry, how will you deal with those feelings now?

JUST

When the Woman saw that the tree looked like good eating and realized what she would get out of it—she'd know everything!—she took and ate the fruit and then gave some to her husband, and he ate.

Immediately the two of them did "see what's really going on"—saw themselves naked! They sewed fig leaves together as makeshift clothes for themselves.

When they heard the sound of GOD strolling in the garden in the evening breeze, the Man and his Wife hid in the trees of the garden, hid from GOD. . . .

[GOD] told the Woman:
"I'll multiply your pains in
        childbirth;
    you'll give birth to your
        babies in pain.
You'll want to please your
        husband,
    but he'll lord it over you."

He told the Man:
"Because you listened to
        your wife
    and ate from the tree
That I commanded you not
        to eat from,
    'Don't eat from this tree,'
The very ground is cursed
        because of you;
    getting food from the
        ground
Will be as painful as having
        babies is for your wife;
    you'll be working in pain
        all your life long.
The ground will sprout
        thorns and weeds,
    you'll get your food the
        hard way,

BIBLE READING

Planting and tilling and
    harvesting,
    sweating in the fields from
    dawn to dusk,
Until you return to that
    ground yourself, dead
    and buried;
    you started out as dirt,
    you'll end up dirt."

//REFLECT

God's love presents only half the picture of His character. He is also holy and just. He will always do what is right, and those who do wrong will get what they deserve. His justice isn't blind. It sees through every pretense and clever argument. Nor can this Judge be bribed. No one can buy his way into God's good graces.

God's justice gives us both comfort and pain. When we look at the state of the world, a condition brought on by the events of Genesis 3, we find hope in knowing that one day God will judge sin once and for all. But His justice also inflicts within us the pain of guilt. Even as we long for God to give the bad guys what they deserve, we know deep down that if God punished every sinner, we too would die. We don't want God to show us His justice. Most of us prefer mercy.

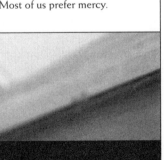

JUST

ACTION

//MICAH 6:6-8

How can I stand up before GOD
and show proper respect to
the high God?
Should I bring an armload of
offerings
topped off with yearling
calves?
Would GOD be impressed with
thousands of rams,
with buckets and barrels of
olive oil?
Would he be moved if I sacrificed
my firstborn child,
my precious baby, to cancel
my sin?

But he's already made it plain
how to live, what to do,
what GOD is looking for in
men and women.
It's quite simple: Do what is fair
and just to your neighbor,
be compassionate and loyal in
your love,
And don't take yourself too
seriously—
take God seriously.

//ACT

Third Street Promenade, Santa Monica, California—the perfect setting to try out this verse. God says He doesn't want my sacrifices; He wants me to do what is just and fair and show my neighbor compassion. Shouldn't be too hard. I walk down the promenade. Street performers excite the crowds around me, and families, couples, and kids laugh at the monkey on a leash or stop to clap for the dancers. I can love these people. They are different from me, no doubt about it, so I stop and throw a dollar into one of their buckets. Done. This verse is easier to act on than I expected. Now on to the street people. I walk into Burger King, buy a cheeseburger, and approach a woman who is talking to herself. "Are you hungry?" I ask. My question hangs in the air unanswered. I leave the cheeseburger on the seat next to her and, dusting off my hands, walk away.

I've done what God wanted. Or have I?

Feeding the homeless and supporting street artists are good things to do. But I wonder what it means to stand up for oppressed people I know personally. Exemplifying God's justice means standing up for the kid who constantly gets picked on at school, fighting for the rights of aborted babies, or confronting someone who is struggling with anorexia. It means getting my hands dirty.

Look around. Where do you see a need for God's justice? Do you see the oppressed around you who need a champion? God doesn't want your sacrifices. He wants you to uphold justice. Now what will you do?

Nicole Davidson
Age: 21
Major: communications

JUST

"Trivialize even the smallest item in God's Law and you will only have trivialized yourself. But take it seriously, show the way for others, and you will find honor in the kingdom. Unless you do far better than the Pharisees in the matters of right living, you won't know the first thing about entering the kingdom."

//REFLECT

Growing up in a culture that revolves around earning what you deserve or working your way to the top is frightening. The Pharisees applied this approach to God. They thought they could earn an eternal reward. People still think that today. Understanding grace in a world that offers so little is difficult.

PRAYER & SOLITUDE

O God, sometimes I find it daunting that I can't buy or bargain my way into Your graces, that I can't rely on sucking up to You to get what I want. You aren't concerned with how much I tithe or whether I attend a Christian school. These aren't the issues that are closest to Your heart.

There have been times when I've caught myself thinking I'm a good Christian, that I set a better religious example than the people around me. When did I become a Pharisee? The hard truth is that there's no faking it with You, God. You've made perfectly clear what You expect from me, and when that Day of Judgment comes, You won't be looking at my nice Christian acts or the WWJD sticker on my car. You'll look at the relationship I have with Your Son, Jesus Christ, and the way I've followed Him into the streets to serve the lost and poor on earth.

I pray that I will fully grasp that Your love and forgiveness aren't given in exchange for good works but that my only hope is Your grace found in Jesus. I pray that I will never be a "Sunday Christian." Make the awe and humility inside of me evident to everyone I meet.

Courtney Harrison
Age: 20
Major: communications

JUST

//ROMANS 3:25-26

God sacrificed Jesus on the altar of the world to clear that world of sin. Having faith in him sets us in the clear. God decided on this course of action in full view of the public—to set the world in the clear with himself through the sacrifice of Jesus, finally taking care of the sins he had so patiently endured. This is not only clear, but it's *now*—this is current history! God sets things right. He also makes it possible for us to live in his rightness.

PRAISE & CELEBRATION

//REFLECT

God should be out of our reach. We are so sinful that He shouldn't even look at us. We are unworthy of His grace. But Paul tells us in Romans that God is in fact within our reach. He's made it possible for us to live in His righteousness, in His light—Christ. This is the beauty of God's loving, merciful judgment. He can't stand to have us separated from Him because of our sin. And for that reason He sacrificed His Son. Can you believe it? *His Son*. Sometimes I've had a hard time sacrificing just ten minutes to pray to God and acknowledge His presence in my life. Yet He sacrificed His Son for all of the filthy sins I have committed and ever will commit. Instead of punishing me, I am *justified* through Christ. Wow!

//PRAISE

My knees buckle at the thought of all God sacrificed for me. When I stop and think about how much it cost Him to bring me into His presence, I don't know what to say in return. But I can start with "Thank you." Then I can give myself to Christ in gratitude for the forgiveness of my every sin—past, present, and future. And then what? What will I give God to show my appreciation for this gift, this sacrifice of His Son? What about you? How will you show your appreciation for the lengths God went for you?

//PRAY

I am forever grateful for God's mercy and forgiveness. I will thank Him always because He loves me and because He made me right with Him. He is awesome, and I want to mirror His merciful judgment. I pray that I'll remember the sacrifice He made and that I'll sacrifice myself for Jesus every day.

Leslie Joy Randleman
Age: 20
Majors: communications; psychology

JUST

Real religion, the kind that passes muster before God the Father, is this: Reach out to the homeless and loveless in their plight, and guard against corruption from the godless world.

FASTING

I'd love to be more involved with helping the poor, but I never see any needy people in my neighborhood. I think loving the "loveless in their plight" is the right thing to do, but that doesn't mean I'll give them another thought or lose sleep over it. My jaded attitude may sound like a stretch, but if you're honest with yourself, how far is it from the truth? Sure, we all say we're gung ho for helping the hungry, sick, and oppressed, but when was the last time I lifted a finger or even thought about those who aren't as blessed as I am? Is it really fair that I live in a beautiful house, never want for a meal, drive my own car, watch cable TV, enjoy hot water in my shower, and have air conditioning on a hot summer day? What did I do to deserve all of this? And why do I always want more?

//FAST

If we could trade places with the homeless and loveless in their plight for a day, maybe they would stop being invisible to us. And that's your assignment for today. Although you can't completely trade places, you can do without the privileges we take for granted. For the next twenty-four hours, live as though you (or your parents) don't have a regular income. Eat only one meal and make it simple and inexpensive. Have something such as a small plate of beans or whatever they're serving tonight at the local rescue mission. No cell phone. No Internet. No computer (unless you absolutely have to finish an assignment). No instant messaging. No e-mail. No television. No hot water. Walk or take public transportation wherever you need to go. If it's summer, don't turn on your air conditioner; if it's winter, keep the heat as low as possible without letting the pipes freeze and sleep with your thinnest blanket. And try doing without that comfy bed by sleeping on the floor.

After fasting from your privileged life for one day, can you now see the homeless and loveless?

Rochelle Renee Veturis
Age: 22
Major: communications

JUST

//MY FOCUS: MATTHEW 22:37-40

Jesus said, "'Love the Lord your God with all your passion and prayer and intelligence.' This is the most important, the first on any list. But there is a second to set alongside it: 'Love others as well as you love yourself.' These two commands are pegs; everything in God's Law and the Prophets hangs from them."

MY JOURNEY

//MY GOD

Much of the secular world views Christians as unapproachable, intolerant, and unforgiving. We talk about loving our neighbor, yet we turn away those who need love—those who need Jesus Christ. Jesus hung out with prostitutes, alcoholics, and liars. He healed them and gave them Himself, the Bread of Life.

All God truly asks is that we love Him and love our neighbors as ourselves. I think we get so caught up in making sure our outfits match and doing what's cool that we forget about those around us. We want to fit in so badly that instead of loving others as ourselves, we put them down just to be accepted by the cool group. How many times do you make fun of others because they dress differently than you? How many times do you pass by a kid at your school who sits alone at the lunch table every day? We're so selfish, even when we do something for someone else. I'll help someone else as long as I get something in return.

What does God think of all this?

//MY THOUGHTS

- Would I still be happy if I were to lose all my possessions? Why or why not?
- What steps will I take to forget about myself and love other people?

Heather Linsday
Age: 21
Major: communications

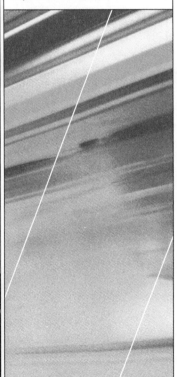

//MY PRAYER

Abba, Papa, I pray that I would learn what love is and practice it daily. I pray that I can forget about myself and concentrate on how I can help those around me. Force me out of my comfort zone to love people without worrying what I'll get out of it. Help me realize that money can't buy happiness and that material things don't last. I pray that I will strive to honor You in all I do.

//JOURNALING: ISAIAH 9:7

His ruling authority will grow,
    and there'll be no limits to the
        wholeness he brings.
He'll rule from the historic
    David throne
    over that promised kingdom.
He'll put that kingdom on a firm
    footing
    and keep it going
With fair dealing and right living,
    beginning now and lasting
        always.
The zeal of GOD-of-the-Angel-
    Armies
    will do all this.

God promises to bring ultimate
justice to this earth. What does
He want you to do today to make
this a reality? How has He opened
your eyes this week to the need
for justice?

MERCIFUL

One day long ago, GOD's Word came to Jonah, Amittai's son: "Up on your feet and on your way to the big city of Nineveh! Preach to them. They're in a bad way and I can't ignore it any longer."

But Jonah got up and went the other direction to Tarshish, running away from GOD. He went down to the port of Joppa and found a ship headed for Tarshish. He paid the fare and went on board, joining those going to Tarshish—as far away from GOD as he could get.

But GOD sent a huge storm at sea, the waves towering. . . .

The men tried rowing back to shore. They made no headway. The storm only got worse and worse, wild and raging.

Then they prayed to GOD, "O GOD! Don't let us drown because of this man's life, and don't blame us for his death. You are GOD. Do what you think is best."

They took Jonah and threw him overboard. Immediately the sea was quieted down.

The sailors were impressed, no longer terrified by the sea, but in awe of GOD. They worshiped GOD, offered a sacrifice, and made vows.

Then GOD assigned a huge fish to swallow Jonah. Jonah was in the fish's belly three days and nights.

BIBLE READING

//REFLECT

Jonah was a prophet, a man who speaks for God. And God sent Him to speak in Nineveh, the Assyrian capital city, which was located in present-day Mosul, Iraq. But Jonah didn't want to go. The Assyrians were vicious, bloodthirsty, idol-worshiping savages who never showed mercy to anyone. As a prophet of the one true God, Jonah found everything about Nineveh offensive. He didn't want to warn the people about God's coming judgment because he was afraid they might listen, turn to God, and be forgiven. Instead, he hoped the Assyrians would get what they had coming for all the pain they'd inflicted on others.

God wanted to warn the Assyrians to show them His mercy, not His judgment. God showed Jonah the same mercy when He didn't let His prophet run away. God chased Jonah down. Why would He do this? Why would God pursue someone who didn't want to obey Him? What does this say about the mercy God still shows people today?

MERCIFUL

Then Jonah prayed to his God from the belly of the fish. He prayed:

"In trouble, deep trouble, I
        prayed to GOD.
    He answered me.
From the belly of the grave I
        cried, 'Help!'
    You heard my cry.
You threw me into ocean's
        depths,
    into a watery grave,
With ocean waves, ocean
        breakers
    crashing over me.
I said, 'I've been thrown away,
    thrown out, out of your
        sight.
I'll never again lay eyes

on your Holy Temple.'
Ocean gripped me by the
        throat.
    The ancient Abyss grabbed
        me and held tight.
My head was all tangled in
        seaweed
    at the bottom of the sea
        where the mountains
        take root.
I was as far down as a body
        can go,
    and the gates were slamming
        shut behind me
        forever—
Yet you pulled me up from that
        grave alive,
    O GOD, my God!
When my life was slipping
        away,

PRAISE & CELEBRATION

//REFLECT

The thing that stands out about Jonah's prayer and praise session from inside a giant fish somewhere in the Mediterranean Sea is the timing. He started singing God's praises while he was still *inside* the fish. God had his attention, and Jonah didn't know how his adventure would turn out. But there was one thing he did know: There is only one God. And that one God had shown him more mercy than he deserved. That led Jonah to worship Him even before he saw the end result of God's plan.

I remembered GOD,
And my prayer got through to you,
  made it all the way to your Holy Temple.
Those who worship hollow gods, god-frauds,
  walk away from their only true love.
But I'm worshiping you, GOD,
  calling out in thanksgiving!
And I'll do what I promised I'd do!
  Salvation belongs to GOD!"

Then GOD spoke to the fish, and it vomited up Jonah on the seashore.

//WORSHIP

All of us go through hard times. We are often like Jonah, bringing the hard times on ourselves through our bad choices. Don't wait for the silver lining to show up. Spend time thanking God and praising Him for His mercy right now. Even if your worst-case scenarios come true, God will still be there. That doesn't mean you will never suffer because of your choices. However, if you do suffer, God's mercy will still cover you. Praise Him for that today.

MERCIFUL

I'm stuck on the part that states, "GOD spoke to Jonah a second time." God called Jonah to go to Nineveh. Did he obey? Did he, a prophet of Yahweh, follow the direction of his God? No. Not the first time. We all know the story. We all know that Jonah messed up, was sentenced to the belly of a big fish, and was given a second chance.

To be honest, I've always thought of Jonah as, well, a prideful idiot. He was a prophet called by God to guide the people of his land. He couldn't exactly run away from this calling. Yet he did. He turned his back and decided that his agenda was better than God's.

If I am going to be perfectly honest, I need to admit that the more I think about Jonah, the more I realize I am like him. Have I decided my way was better even though God told me to do something else? Have I chosen to grab the reins of my life and go my

//MY FOCUS: JONAH 3:1-2

Next, GOD spoke to Jonah a second time: "Up on your feet and on your way to the big city of Nineveh! Preach to them. They're in a bad way and I can't ignore it any longer."

MY JOURNEY

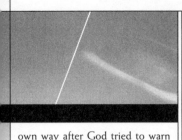

own way after God tried to warn me about a relationship and told me to avoid a precarious situation? And moreover, did God answer me when I was overwhelmed by those circumstances? Did He pull me out and bring me back home? Yes, yes, and yes.

The real story is not Jonah being swallowed by the fish. It's the God of Jonah granting him a second chance. This story that many of us have heard since childhood has a message we simply do not grasp. God's mercy is why we are here, why we have the freedom to try again. If we claim to have a merciful God, why don't we think of Him that way?

//MY PRAYER

Abba, I want to understand the depth of Your mercy. I don't understand why You give me a second chance, and sometimes I don't even understand why I need a second chance—and a third and a fourth and more. Abba, break this prideful heart. May I know deep within my soul that it's not about me; it's about You and Your mercy for this broken soul.

//MY THOUGHTS

- In whom do I put my trust? Why?
- Do I believe I will receive God's mercy? Why or why not?
- Do I believe I can trust His mercy? Why or why not?

Corrie Brazell
Age: 20
Major: English

MERCIFUL

ACTION

//JONAH 3:3-5

This time Jonah started off straight for Nineveh, obeying GOD's orders to the letter.

Nineveh was a big city, very big—it took three days to walk across it.

Jonah entered the city, went one day's walk and preached, "In forty days Nineveh will be smashed."

The people of Nineveh listened, and trusted God. They proclaimed a citywide fast and dressed in burlap to show their repentance. Everyone did it—rich and poor, famous and obscure, leaders and followers.

//REFLECT

We all know people we think would never listen to anything about God. In our eyes, they are too far gone. If we walked over to them and told them something to the effect of, "Jesus died for you," we think they would laugh in our faces. Who would possibly want to subject herself to that kind of embarrassment?

This is how Jonah felt about the people of Nineveh. In his mind, the whole missionary excursion was a huge waste of time. No one would listen, as least he hoped no one would. He probably thought he would be lucky to get out of the town alive. But, to his chagrin, they did listen. From the poorest beggar on the street to the king in his palace, the people listened and turned to God.

//ACT

Risk the embarrassment and go talk to your "unreachables." Tell them how Jesus changed your life and how He can change their lives as well. Don't worry about how they might react. Offer them God's mercy. Who knows? They might pull a Nineveh on you and turn to God. Even if they don't, you'll have done exactly what God wants you to do. After all, if you don't tell these people about God's mercy, who will?

MERCIFUL

//JONAH 3:10-4:2

God saw what they had done, that they had turned away from their evil lives. He *did* change his mind about them. What he said he would do to them he didn't do. Jonah was furious. He lost his temper. He yelled at GOD, "GOD! I knew it—when I was back home, I knew this was going to happen! That's why I ran off to Tarshish! I knew you were sheer grace and mercy, not easily angered, rich in love, and ready at the drop of a hat to turn your plans of punishment into a program of forgiveness!"

//REFLECT

I understand that You are merciful. This is something I heard proclaimed even before I was a Christian. I just don't understand why.

Why, God? Why are You so gracious and merciful to Your children and to me in particular? I'm ashamed to admit it, but I consciously do things that I shouldn't do. I realize that I shouldn't drink, but I do it anyway. I know that I shouldn't be angry toward my parents, but I'm angry anyway. I know that I shouldn't look down on people

PRAYER & SOLITUDE

//PRAY

Papa, what's wrong with me? I know the answer to that one. I'm a sinner who will always fall short of glorifying You. Please guide me. Guide me always to do what You ask of me. I know I won't always get it right, but teach me not to take advantage of Your mercy. I love You. I want to show You I love You in whatever way I can. Teach me. Amen.

who are homeless, but I do it anyway. I hate being like this. I really do.

I ask why You are so merciful to Your children, but I honestly don't want to know. I'm just grateful that You are. I'm grateful that You still forgive me despite all the wrong things I have done and continue to do.

I wonder, *Are all Christians as inconsistent as I am?*

//THINK

- What do my actions say about my claim to love God?
- If I say I love God but still do things I shouldn't, am I taking advantage of His mercy? How?
- Will there come a point when God's patience with me will run out? How do I know?

Vanessa Salazar
Age: 20
Major: communications

MERCIFUL

GOD said, "What do you have to be angry about?"

But Jonah just left. He went out of the city to the east and sat down in a sulk. He put together a makeshift shelter of leafy branches and sat there in the shade to see what would happen to the city.

GOD arranged for a broad-leafed tree to spring up. It grew over Jonah to cool him off and get him out of his angry sulk. Jonah was pleased and enjoyed the shade. Life was looking up.

FASTING

But then God sent a worm. By dawn of the next day, the worm had bored into the shade tree and it withered away. The sun came up and God sent a hot, blistering wind from the east. The sun beat down on Jonah's head and he started to faint. He prayed to die: "I'm better off dead!"

Then God said to Jonah, "What right do you have to get angry about this shade tree?"

Jonah said, "Plenty of right. It's made me angry enough to die!"

GOD said, "What's this? How is it that you can change your feelings from pleasure to anger overnight about a mere shade tree that you did nothing to get? You neither planted nor watered it. It grew up one night and died the next night. So, why can't I likewise change what I feel about Nineveh from anger to pleasure, this big city of more than a hundred

//FAST

and twenty thousand childlike people who don't yet know right from wrong, to say nothing of all the innocent animals?"

Jonah was angry because he wanted everyone in Nineveh to get zapped by God. When God forgave them instead, it ticked him off. Jonah's plant episode showed he cared more about his own comfort than about people made in God's image. In a word, he was judgmental.

Who in your life do you have the same attitude toward? They may be individuals who hurt you or people you can't stand because of the color of their skin or the way they dress. Who wouldn't you mind seeing a little fire falling from the sky on top of their heads? Spend time praying for these people today. Don't entertain judgmental thoughts, even for a second. Instead, do whatever you can to show them God's mercy. God loves them, even if you don't.

//JOURNALING: JONAH 2:8

Those who worship hollow
gods, god-frauds,
walk away from their only
true love.

The book of Jonah paints a sharp
contrast between God and Jonah.
God loves. Forgives. And pours
out His mercy. Jonah hates. Holds
grudges. And demands revenge.
So who are you like, God or
Jonah? Here's a little hint: If God
asks you to forgive someone or tell
that person about Him but you
refuse, you've just pulled a Jonah.
If God is so merciful, how should
you live? Have you withheld
God's mercy from those who are
dying to receive it?

TRUTHFUL

//PSALM 19:7-14, JOHN 17:17, AND JOHN 18:38

PSALM 19:7-14

The revelation of GOD is whole
  and pulls our lives together.
The signposts of GOD are clear
  and point out the right road.
The life-maps of GOD are right,
  showing the way to joy.
The directions of GOD are plain
  and easy on the eyes.
GOD's reputation is twenty-
  four-carat gold,
  with a lifetime guarantee.
The decisions of GOD are
  accurate
  down to the nth degree.

God's Word is better than a
  diamond,
  better than a diamond set
    between emeralds.
You'll like it better than
  strawberries in spring,
  better than red, ripe
    strawberries.

There's more: God's Word
  warns us of danger
and directs us to hidden
  treasure.
Otherwise how will we find our
  way?
  Or know when we play the
    fool?
Clean the slate, God, so we can
  start the day fresh!
  Keep me from stupid sins,
  from thinking I can take over
    your work;
Then I can start this day sun-
  washed,
  scrubbed clean of the grime
    of sin.
These are the words in my
  mouth;
  these are what I chew on and
    pray.
Accept them when I place them
  on the morning altar,
O God, my Altar-Rock,
  God, Priest-of-My-Altar.

BIBLE READING

JOHN 17:17

"Make them holy—
    consecrated—with the
    truth;
Your word is consecrating
truth."

JOHN 18:38

Pilate said, "What is truth?"

God never lies. He lives and tells the truth. We can trust Him absolutely. But what is truth? How does God's truthfulness reveal itself in a culture that doesn't believe in the existence of truth? And what difference will His truth make in our everyday lives? Saying we believe that God's Word is true is easy. The real test comes when we try to live our belief in a culture that dismisses every claim to absolute truth as nothing more than ramblings of religious fanatics.

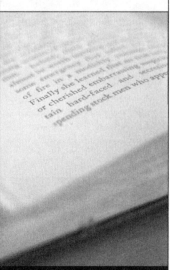

TRUTHFUL

ACTION

//1 JOHN 3:18-19

My dear children, let's not just talk about love; let's practice real love. This is the only way we'll know we're living truly, living in God's reality.

//REFLECT

The Bible tells us that truth is a belt around our waists and a light unto our paths. The Holy Spirit reveals it, guilt is banished through it, love rejoices in it. The father of lies distorts it, Jesus is it, and there's not a thing we can do about it. We do not deserve it, we will not earn it, and we cannot hide from it. Truth is a promise: If we ask, seek, and knock, we will experience it, and it will make us free. Psalm 85:10 says, "Love and Truth meet in the street." That's God's mysterious reality. Truth will lead you straight into the arms of Love, where He's waiting for you to join Him there in the street.

//ACT

Knowing where truth can be found is not enough. We have to seek it and find it. Some of us don't want to look because we know where it'll lead us—into the street with God, showing love to the unlovable. Others are just too lazy to look. We think it's enough to meet God in the street without worrying about something as elusive as truth. It's not. Truth *and* love meet in the street. You have to have both.

Start the search for truth today. Pick a book of the Bible and read it from beginning to end. Choose one you've never read before and don't limit yourself to a short book such as Philemon or Jude. Read a book such as Romans or the gospel of John from the first verse to the last. As you do, pray over and over, *Holy Spirit of the living God, guide me in Your truth.*

If there's one thought in this mess of words to tattoo on your forehead, it's this: When we really look for truth, we'll find it after we give up our preconceived notions of what we want it to be. Society's expectations, the church's traditions, our parents' demands, and our own dreams all fall to the floor as truth moves us toward real Love.

Jana Woods
Age: 20
Major: communications

TRUTHFUL

//PROVERBS 12:16-18

Fools have short fuses and
    explode all too quickly;
    the prudent quietly shrug off
    insults.

Truthful witness by a good
    person clears the air,
    but liars lay down a smoke
    screen of deceit.

Rash language cuts and maims,
    but there is healing in the
    words of the wise.

//REFLECT

For me, the hardest place to
wrestle with God is in an arena
filled with Christians. I know that
everyone doubts at some point, but
part of me walks around thinking
everyone else is A-OK with God.
They talk to Him every day, have
quiet times every night, and are
best friends with the Almighty. I
wish I were like them.

Instead, I struggle with faith,
but I hide behind a mask that
makes people think I have a great
relationship with God. Deep
inside I know the Bible tells me to
be like God and be truthful. Am
I being honest when I wear my
mask of Christianity? Or am I just
making things harder for myself?
Do I dare come clean and speak
the truth about my spiritual life? If
I did, would I find others out there
just like me?

//FAST

I pray that I can be honest with myself and with others about who God is in my life. Today I will try to make my prayers a reality. I'm going to fast from hypocrisy and take off my mask for the day. No more pretending I have some great relationship with God when in reality I struggle with doubt. How can I ever find answers to life's biggest questions—questions of life and death and why we live this life anyway—when I pretend I already know them?

I invite you to join me in my mask-free day. Get honest with God and yourself. Stop pretending you have it all together. Let people see your struggle. Who knows, you may find someone out there who's already been through this wrestling match and survived the experience. Your getting real may allow that person to help you through to the other side without giving up on God altogether.

Alaia Williams
Age: 20
Major: communications

TRUTHFUL

Investigate my life, O God,
    find out everything about me;
Cross-examine and test me,
    get a clear picture of what I'm
        about;
See for yourself whether I've
        done anything wrong—
    then guide me on the road to
        eternal life.

PRAISE & CELEBRATION

//REFLECT

Do I want to hear the truth? Nobody likes a liar. But then again, sometimes a lie is easier to hear than the truth. Like when you get dressed up for a special occasion. Maybe you spend hours picking out clothes and making yourself look just right. And you ask, "How do I look?" Don't you just want to hear, "You look great!"?

Do you think sometimes we go to God like that? We go to Him in worship and act as if everything is just fine between us, but it's not. We sing and smile and do all the right things on the outside, but on the inside—well, that's another story. But do we really want God to tell us the truth about what's going on? Do we really want Him to tell it like it is? Either way, He will. God is always truthful. That's all He knows how to be. Truth isn't just what He says. Truth is what He is.

It's true that worship is all about God, but it's about my heart as well. Worship is about communication between God and me. I'm telling God what's true about Him as I sing to Him. Do I want Him to reciprocate?

A lie may be easier to hear, but with God, lying isn't an option. If God tells us something we don't want to hear, are we ready to make a change? What if we're in the middle of singing a heartfelt song and the Holy Spirit challenges us with questions such as, *Do you really mean this?* or *Are you prepared to make that statement?* How will we respond? Are we ready to hear the truth about ourselves? Are we ready to hear the truth about Him?

//PRAISE

Go to God and ask Him to show you any lies you believe about yourself. Ask Him to show you the truth, no matter the cost. Let Him rip away the lies so you can worship Him in Spirit and in *truth* (see John 4:23-24). Then worship Him with the freedom complete honesty brings.

Ross King, contributing editor

TRUTHFUL

Peter said, "I don't get it. Put it in plain language."

Jesus replied, "You too? Are you being willfully stupid? Don't you know that anything that is swallowed works its way through the intestines and is finally defecated? But what comes out of the mouth gets its start in the heart. It's from the heart that we vomit up evil arguments, murders, adulteries, fornications, thefts, lies, and cussing."

MY JOURNEY

//MY GOD

You want the truth. Well, okay, truth scares me. Honestly, I want to give in to temptation, and I have many times. Being completely honest is scary because it means I am responsible for the truth and therefore for everything I do. The truth is that I have nothing to blame my evil doings on except my own desire. That's scary!

Before truth, I could blame anything for my evil: "My friends influenced me to drink. Television said that sex was okay. That book on etiquette taught me to lie." But no! Now the truth says that *I* am to blame? That my evil is my *own* fault? That I *chose* it? Funny, I don't remember choosing evil. On that career aptitude test I took in ninth grade, I didn't bubble in *Liar*. No, because answering that on a test would have been brutal honesty.

Just because we grow up with evil influences around us, we shouldn't use them as an excuse to succumb

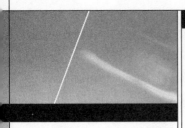

//MY PRAYER

God, I pray that You would help me hold myself accountable to Your truth. I pray that I would fear You more and remain in awe of Your awesome love. I also pray that I would fear the truth less and openly embrace complete honesty—with myself, with others, and most important with You.

to our own desires. If we're honest with ourselves, we might see the truth: We choose evil every day in some form. It's called sin. And Jesus died to set us free from it. How can we blame God for tempting us when along with the capacity for evil He's given us the capacity for truth? What we do with truth is completely up to us. Now *that's* scary.

//MY THOUGHTS

- How much time have I spent blaming others for my own sins? What will I do to use this time more effectively?
- In what areas of my life have I been afraid to be honest with myself?

Rebecca Turner
Age: 18
Major: communications

TRUTHFUL

//JAMES 1:13-15

Don't let anyone under pressure to give in to evil say, "God is trying to trip me up." God is impervious to evil, and puts evil in no one's way. The temptation to give in to evil comes from us and only us. We have no one to blame but the leering, seducing flare-up of our own lust. Lust gets pregnant, and has a baby: sin! Sin grows up to adulthood, and becomes a real killer.

//PRAY

God, I find that it's easy to blame You for my sin. I'm struggling to find friends, so I've started drinking to fit in better. Whose fault is this? Yours, God—You should've given me friends before I became this desperate. My parents are in the middle of a divorce, and I started smoking marijuana to cope with it. Whose fault is this? Yours, God—You should make my parents get along. I had sex with my boyfriend to prove that I love him. Now I'm pregnant. Whose fault is this? Yours, God—no one else gets pregnant the first time.

PRAYER & SOLITUDE

//THINK

- Do I take responsibility for my actions, or do I try to blame God and others for my poor choices? Why?
- When I allow my circumstances rather than the truth of God's Word to dictate my feelings toward God, what should I do?

Jessi Boicelli
Age: 18
Major: journalism

Then I hear James tell me that You don't put evil in my way. I sin because some part of me wants to sin. Things don't always go my way, but they don't for anyone. You don't deceive me. You set the truth in front of me. Help me to walk in Your truth rather than make lame excuses for my actions. O Father, keep my desires from leading me to sin. Let me endure the hard times through the fellowship of other believers who will help me. And in my good times, let me be a friend to those who are going through something difficult. Remind me that the rough times make the good times much sweeter. Thank You so much for giving me real life in You.

//JOURNALING: HEBREWS 6:17-18

When God wanted to guarantee his promises, he gave his word, a rock-solid guarantee—God *can't* break his word. And because his word cannot change, the promise is likewise unchangeable.

God never breaks His promises. His Word is always the truth. Because you are supposed to be like Him, truth should permeate everything you say and do. Does it? Why or why not? How do you need to change to bring your life in line with His truth?

DAY

1

2

3

4

5

6

7

FAITHFUL

NUMBERS 23:19

God is not man, one given to
lies,
   and not a son of man
      changing his mind.
Does he speak and not do what
   he says?
   Does he promise and not
      come through?

EXODUS 34:4-7

So Moses cut two tablets of
stone just like the originals. He
got up early in the morning and
climbed Mount Sinai as GOD
had commanded him, carrying
the two tablets of stone. GOD
descended in the cloud and took
up his position there beside him
and called out the name, GOD.
GOD passed in front of him and
called out, "GOD, GOD, a God
of mercy and grace, endlessly
patient—so much love, so
deeply true—loyal in love for a
thousand generations, forgiving
iniquity, rebellion, and sin. Still,
he doesn't ignore sin. He holds
sons and grandsons responsible
for a father's sins to the third
and even fourth generation."

2 TIMOTHY 2:13

If we give up on him, he does
   not give up—
   for there's no way he can be
      false to himself.

BIBLE READING

//REFLECT

God is always faithful. He keeps His promises. Always. His faithfulness is the one thing we can count on in an uncertain world. And His faithfulness does not depend on us. That's why we call His love unconditional and why salvation comes through His grace. God extends these promises to us in spite of ourselves. Even after we become Jesus' followers, God's faithfulness exceeds our own. We might struggle with doubt, but God never does. He never doubts us, and He never gives up on us because doing so would mean giving up on Himself.

FAITHFUL

So, what do you think? With God on our side like this, how can we lose?

PRAISE & CELEBRATION

//PRAISE

Let the party begin! God is on our side; we can't lose. So get the celebration going! Instead of walking through life all depressed and filled with doubt and despair, we should be dancing. Sure, we still have trouble. Problems won't leave us alone—at least not until Jesus comes back for us—but they don't matter. Paul put it this way:

If God didn't hesitate to put everything on the line for us, embracing our condition and exposing himself to the worst by sending his own Son, is there anything else he wouldn't gladly and freely do for us? And who would dare tangle with God by messing with one of God's chosen? Who would dare even to point a finger? The One who died for us—who was raised to life for us!—is in the presence of God at this very moment sticking up for us. Do you think anyone is going to be able to drive a wedge between us and Christ's love for us? There is no way! Not trouble, not hard times, not hatred, not hunger, not homelessness, not bullying threats, not back-stabbing, not even the worst sins listed in Scripture:

They kill us in cold blood
    because they hate you.
We're sitting ducks; they pick
    us off one by one.

None of this fazes us because
    Jesus loves us. (Romans
    8:32-37)

So let's celebrate. In fact, life should be one giant celebration of God's love and faithfulness. Let's start rejoicing no matter what we go through. Are you having a bad day? Look at it through the lens of God's faithfulness. He promised to use all your bad days to make you more like Jesus (see James 1:2-4). Does grief have you in its grip? God promised to comfort you and rescue you when you feel as if you're about to die from a broken heart (see Psalm 34:18; 2 Corinthians 1:3-4). Remember, God gave His only Son to save you. He isn't about to abandon you now.

So celebrate!

FAITHFUL

ACTION

//ROMANS 3:4

God keeps his word even when the whole world is lying through its teeth. Scripture says the same:

> Your words stand fast and
>   true;
> Rejection doesn't faze you.

//REFLECT

Why does God pay attention to me? Comparing me to God is like comparing a grain of sand to Mount Everest. I'm human, I'm a sinner, I'm a screwup, and that's the way I'll always be. How will I ever measure up to anything that could be worthy of Him? I've heard over and over again how God loves me enough that He sent His one and only Son to die for me. But why? Why me? Why does God, the Alpha and the Omega, believe so securely in me, especially when I find it hard to believe in myself? If I can't even have faith in myself, how can He?

Maybe I can't understand God's faith in me because I've never invested that much faith in others. Matthew 17:20 says the smallest amount of faith can move mountains—that's huge! I can only imagine what I would be capable of if I had the same amount of faith in myself that God does. The almighty God says that with Him I can do anything. What am I waiting for?

//ACT

Has God told you to do something that you haven't done because of doubt? Maybe He told you to go on a short-term mission trip, but you avoided signing up because you didn't know how you would raise the money to pay for it. Or maybe He told you to give away one of your prized possessions, but you refused because you didn't know how you would live without it. God is faithful, and He has faith in you. He knows you can do the impossible things He asks because He is the One who will make sure they get done.

Today, step out in faith and obey God even if you aren't sure how everything will work out. One word of caution: Make sure your instructions come from God. Don't try to jump off the top of your dorm and fly because you think God will catch you. He won't tell you to do something like that. Instead, listen for the quiet but definite voice of God telling you to get out of your comfort zone, risk failure, and follow Him. What are you waiting for?

Jillian Michelle Cruz
Age: 21
Major: communications with an emphasis in interpersonal/organizational and journalism

FAITHFUL

//LAMENTATIONS 3:19-23

I'll never forget the trouble, the
    utter lostness,
    the taste of ashes, the poison
        I've swallowed.
I remember it all—oh, how well
    I remember—
    the feeling of hitting the
        bottom.
But there's one other thing I
    remember,
    and remembering, I keep a
        grip on hope:

GOD's loyal love couldn't have
    run out,
    his merciful love couldn't have
        dried up.
They're created new every
    morning.
    How great your faithfulness!

//REFLECT

Have you ever felt alone, lost,
confused? Are you going through
a tough time and feel as if there
is no one there to pick up the
broken pieces?

I've had trouble with friends,
family, finances, you name it.
I've felt like Jeremiah felt. I've
been at my lowest when the only
thing I could do was look up and
hope for something better, for
someone to pull me up. During
these times of hopelessness and
despair, Psalm 55:22 encouraged
me. It says,

PRAYER & SOLITUDE

//PRAY

Lord, I need Your help right now. I don't understand why all these things are happening to me. I ask that You would help me to know that even when it feels as if You aren't there, You are. I pray that I would learn what You are trying to teach me.

Pile your troubles on GOD's
    shoulders—
    he'll carry your load, he'll help
        you out.
He'll never let good people
    topple into ruin.

I know that whatever I'm going through, God is there. Even when I can't hear Him or I feel as if He isn't there, God has promised to take care of me. He won't let anything happen to me that is not of His will. God had mercy on His prophet in his time of despair, and God's mercy is never ending.

//THINK

- What am I doing that creates distance between God and me? How will I change that?
- What can I do to make God a part of my day when I feel as if He's not there?

Kimberly Ann McCormick
Age: 21
Major: communications with an emphasis in interpersonal/organizational

FAITHFUL

//1 TIMOTHY 5:12-13 AND LUKE 16:10-12

1 TIMOTHY 5:12-13

By breaking their word, they're liable to go from bad to worse, frittering away their days on empty talk, gossip, and trivialities.

LUKE 16:10-12

"If you're honest in small things, you'll be honest in big things; If you're a crook in small things, you'll be a crook in big things. If you're not honest in small jobs, who will put you in charge of the store?"

//REFLECT

Small things matter. Little things add up, like the money I spend at Starbucks and the time I invest in my PlayStation. Usually I think only some big sin can trip me up, that a big, bad 'Thou shalt not' is what gets in my way of being completely faithful to God. But it's the little things that show where my affections lie. If I spend more time preparing for a fantasy baseball draft than seeking God's direction for my life, then something deep down inside of me isn't right. When the trivial takes priority over the important, my life needs to change.

//FAST

Today, fast from the trivial. For the rest of the day, do without things that don't really matter. Instead of watching a mindless movie or playing solitaire on your computer, use that time to read the Bible and pray. Give the money you would spend on a latte to missions or to someone who wouldn't have a meal otherwise. Find a way to use the money, time, and energy you would normally spend on the trivial to do something important, something that matters, something that will last longer than getting to the second level on Halo 2.

FAITHFUL

//MY FOCUS: 1 CORINTHIANS 1:7-9

Just think—you don't need a thing, you've got it all! All God's gifts are right in front of you as you wait expectantly for our Master Jesus to arrive on the scene for the Finale. And not only that, but God himself is right alongside to keep you steady and on track until things are all wrapped up by Jesus. God, who got you started in this spiritual adventure, shares with us the life of his Son and our Master Jesus. He will never give up on you. Never forget that.

//MY GOD

I'm sitting in church again, listening to another testimony of someone who overcame a struggle and found God in that one moment. Stories like this make me feel as if the Christian life is supposed to be perfect: no problems, only happiness. Every time I sin, I feel like a failure. So I don't speak up when I should, and I live in guilt, wondering if God could ever work through such a shameful piece of trash like me. But there's something I always seem to forget: "He will never give up on [me]."

God loves me and will never abandon me to a mediocre existence. This may be old news to many, but I often forget that God is *for* me. I try to be perfect and forget to learn from my mistakes. Without mistakes, I'd never see how much I need God. My own faith is not perfect and never will be. But God's faithfulness is perfect and will carry me through

MY JOURNEY

//MY THOUGHTS

- If I am doing just enough to get by, what will I change about my life to truly follow God?
- What will I do when God doesn't take away my struggles?

Tim Posada
Age: 22
Major: communications

if I let it. Even when I don't think I can make it, God does. I may be weak, but in my weakness, I become strong through Christ (see 2 Corinthians 12:10).

I can tell myself that my struggle is under God's protection, but until I truly give God control, He will never be able to work through me. First I have to give up my guilt and believe in God's will for me. I must never forget that God is there beside me. He's just waiting for me to notice.

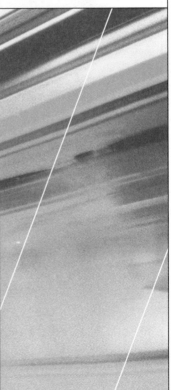

//JOURNALING: PSALM 100:5

For GOD is sheer beauty,
all-generous in love,
loyal always and ever.

God's faithfulness means He will always be loyal to us even when we are disloyal to Him. How should you respond to such faithfulness, to so much love? If God is loyal to you, shouldn't you reciprocate? How will you change your life to show greater faithfulness to Him?

CONTRIBUTORS

Mark Tabb, general editor
> Devotions: those not written by students or the contributing editor
> Author of nine books, including *Greater Than: Unconventional Thoughts on the Infinite God*
> Favorite book: *Loving God* by Charles Colson
> How I will make a difference in the world: by writing books that force people to think

Ross King, contributing editor
> Devotions: Praise & Celebration—Passionate, pages 28–29; Near, pages 68–69; Silent, pages 86–87; and Truthful, pages 126–127
> Worship leader, songwriter, recording artist
> Favorite book: THE LORD OF THE RINGS series by J. R. R. Tolkien
> How I will make a difference in the world: generally, to do the things that Jesus said; specifically, to make good, intelligent art for the glory of God

STUDENT CONTRIBUTORS, AZUSA PACIFIC UNIVERSITY:

Brian Allan
> Devotion: My Journey—Silent, pages 88–89
> Age: 19
> Major: undeclared (maybe art, maybe writing, maybe nothing)
> Favorite book: *The Stranger* by Albert Camus
> How I will make a difference in the world: by being honest

Anonymous
> Devotion: Fasting—Near, pages 74–75

Tiffany Jean BeMent

Devotion: Prayer & Solitude—Creative, pages 10–11

Age: 18

Major: business marketing

Favorite book: *The Sacred Romance* by John Eldredge

How I will make a difference in the world: I hope to change my community by helping inner-city children further their education and eventually have the opportunity to attend a four-year university.

Jessi Boicelli

Devotion: Prayer & Solitude—Truthful, pages 130–131

Age: 18

Major: journalism

Favorite book: *My Name Is Asher Lev* by Chaim Potok

How I will make a difference in the world: by loving people as individuals—as God created us

Corrie Brazell

Devotions: Fasting—Passionate, pages 32–33; My Journey—Merciful, pages 110–111

Age: 20

Major: English

Favorite book: *To Kill a Mockingbird* by Harper Lee

How I will make a difference in the world: by bringing back slap bracelets—they make life more entertaining.

Rebecca Joy Burton

Devotion: Action—Powerful, pages 44–45

Age: 20

Major: communications with an emphasis in journalism

Favorite book: *The Phantom Tollbooth* by Norton Juster

How I will make a difference in the world: I've made very few plans for my life, but I am sure of this: My life will make a difference because God moves in it, and I happen to know that God can do huge anythings with very small somethings.

Caylee Carpenter
> Devotion: My Journey—Creative, pages 18–19
> Age: 18
> Major: psychology
> Favorite book: *Redeeming Love* by Francine Rivers
> How I will make a difference in the world: I would like to establish
> my own place for abused children and provide opportunities for
> them to succeed.

Darrah Christel
> Devotion: Action—Passionate, pages 30–31
> Age: 18
> Major: marketing
> Favorite books: *Memoirs of a Geisha* by Arthur Golden; *Portrait of an
> Artist as a Young Man* by James Joyce
> How I will make a difference in the world: I once heard that life is
> not about breaths we take but the moments that take our breath
> away. I live for those moments.

Adam Cozens
> Devotion: Prayer & Solitude—Powerful, pages 46–47
> Age: 20
> Major: media communications
> Favorite book: *The Gift of Pain* by Philip Yancey and Dr. Paul Brand
> How I will make a difference in the world: I want to make
> Christianity a cool thing rather than something people feel they
> have to hide in order to fit in.

Justin Crutchfield
> Devotion: Prayer & Solitude—Frightening, pages 54–55
> Age: 21
> Majors: cinema; English
> Favorite book: *Of Human Bondage* by W. Somerset Maugham
> How I will make a difference in the world: I want to make at least
> one good movie or documentary.

Jillian Michelle Cruz

Devotion: Action—Faithful, pages 138–139

Age: 21

Major: communications with an emphasis in interpersonal/
organizational and journalism

Favorite book: *Mere Christianity* by C. S. Lewis

How I will make a difference in the world: "You must be the change
you wish to see in the world."—Gandhi

Nicole Davidson

Devotion: Action—Just, pages 94–95

Age: 21

Major: communications

Favorite book: The Bible

How I will make a difference in the world: "Do something today
which the world may talk of hereafter."—Admiral Collingwood

Rachel Fagg

Devotion: Prayer & Solitude—Silent, pages 80–81

Age: 18

Major: liberal studies

Favorite book: *Jane Eyre* by Charlotte Brontë

How I will make a difference in the world: by loving as many
people as I can

Michelle Galloway

Devotion: My Journey—Passionate, pages 26–27

Age: 18

Major: undeclared (probably art)

Favorite book: *Stargirl* by Jerri Spinelli

How I will make a difference in the world: by striving to be just
who God created me to be

Courtney Harrison

>Devotion: Prayer & Solitude—Just, pages 96–97
>
>Age: 20
>
>Major: communications
>
>Favorite book: *Jane Eyre* by Charlotte Brontë
>
>How I will make a difference in the world: by showing those who are hurting that I care about them and so does God. I hope to take any and every opportunity I can to help others and show compassion.

Lindy Hunker

>Devotion: My Journey—Frightening, pages 56–57
>
>Age: 20
>
>Major: communications
>
>Favorite book: anything by Max Lucado
>
>How I will make a difference in the world: I want to change the world one smile at a time.

Christel Kopitzke

>Devotion: Action—Near, pages 66–67
>
>Age: 22
>
>Major: youth ministry
>
>Favorite book: *Messy Spirituality* by Mike Yaconelli
>
>How I will make a difference in the world: one student at a time

Heather Linsday

>Devotion: My Journey—Just, pages 102–103
>
>Age: 21
>
>Major: communications
>
>Favorite book: *The Notebook* by Nicholas Sparks
>
>How I will make a difference in the world: Because of God's unconditional love, I want to show that love to others, viewing them through His eyes.

Kimberly Ann McCormick
   Devotion: Prayer & Solitude—Faithful, pages 140–141
   Age: 21
   Major: communications with an emphasis in interpersonal/
      organizational
   Favorite books: *Jane Eyre* by Charlotte Brontë; *My Utmost for His
      Highest* by Oswald Chambers
   How I will make a difference in the world: by exhibiting Christ's
      character as a daughter, sister, friend, athlete, businessperson,
      and eventually as a wife and mother

Tim Posada
   Devotion: My Journey—Faithful, pages 144–145
   Age: 22
   Major: communications
   Favorite book: *Diary* by Chuck Palahniuk
   How I will make a difference in the world: I hope to bring about
      change by helping people be able to laugh at themselves more.

Emily Radonich
   Devotion: Fasting—Silent, pages 82–83
   Age: 18
   Major: business administration
   Favorite book: *The Count of Monte Cristo* by Alexandre Dumas
   How I will make a difference in the world: I want to make people
      smile.

Leslie Joy Randleman
   Devotions: My Journey—Powerful, pages 42–43; Praise &
      Celebration—Just, pages 98–99
   Age: 20
   Majors: communications; psychology
   Favorite book: *Blue Like Jazz* by Donald Miller
   How I will make a difference in the world: by first making a
      difference in myself (see Romans 12:2) so that others may do
      the same

Diana Robles

Devotion: Action—Silent, pages 84–85

Age: 19

Major: psychology

Favorite book: *Little Women* by Louisa May Alcott

How I will make a difference in the world: Just like Oprah, I plan to become successful so I have the resources to go to other countries and take care of starving, orphaned, and sick children.

Vanessa Salazar

Devotion: Prayer & Solitude—Merciful, pages 114–115

Age: 20

Major: communications

Favorite book: *The Scarlet Letter* by Nathaniel Hawthorne

How I will make a difference in the world: Getting involved with mainstream radio stations will allow me to represent Christians and Christ in a way that screams, "I'm not perfect! I never will be, but I love Jesus Christ and I devote my life to Him."

Amy Joy Serry

Devotion: Prayer & Solitude—Near, pages 70–71

Age: 22

Major: chemistry

Favorite book: anything by C. S. Lewis

How I will make a difference in the world: I want to make a difference in my little corner of the world by using my eclectic talents to proclaim God's glory as it is revealed in creation.

Carrie Taylor

Devotion: My Journey—Near, pages 72–73

Age: 21

Major: communications with an emphasis in journalism; cognate in writing and editing

Favorite book: *The Voyage of the Dawn Treader* by C. S. Lewis

How I will make a difference in the world: by making chocolate one of the essential food groups

Jennifer Tibbett

    Devotion: Prayer & Solitude — Passionate, pages 24–25

    Age: 18

    Major: English

    Favorite book: *The Wind in the Willows* by Kenneth Grahame

    How I will make a difference in the world: "What wisdom can you
        find that is greater than kindness?"—Jean-Jacques Rousseau

Rebecca Turner

    Devotion: My Journey — Truthful, pages 128–129

    Age: 18

    Major: communications

    Favorite book: *A Prayer for Owen Meany* by John Irving

    How I will make a difference in the world: by being the best person
        I can be

Rochelle Renee Veturis

    Devotion: Fasting — Just, pages 100–101

    Age: 22

    Major: communications

    Favorite book: *Gone with the Wind* by Margaret Mitchell

    How I will make a difference in the world: by honoring God to the
        best of my ability and by smiling at people

Andrew Wheeler

    Devotion: Action — Frightening, pages 52–53

    Age: 20

    Major: communications with an emphasis in journalism

    Favorite book: THE LORD OF THE RINGS series by J. R. R. Tolkien

    How I will make a difference in the world: by just being myself. I
        figure if you have to be someone else to change the world, the
        world may not be worth changing.

Alaia Williams
Devotion: Fasting—Truthful, pages 124–125
Age: 20
Major: communications
Favorite book: *Living Buddha, Living Christ* by Thich Nhat Hanh
How I will make a difference in the world: by being actively
involved in the community and using my gifts, talents, and
resources to not only support myself but also to help and
support others

Jana Woods
Devotion: Action—Truthful, pages 122–123
Age: 20
Major: communications
Favorite books: *The Ragamuffin Gospel* by Brennan Manning; *Simple Path* by Mother Teresa
How I will make a difference in the world: I've learned to not
make plans. I only hope to always learn new ways and reasons
to love my Maker and to love living no matter where, when,
or to whom mystery draws this ragamuffin. I expect that to be
influential in and of itself, and I think it's enough.